A FAMILY AFFAIR

A FAMILY AFFAIR

The Margaret and Tony Story

Roger Hutchinson
and
Gary Kahn

Two Continents
Bunch Books

Library of Congress Cataloging in Publication Data
Hutchinson, Roger
  A family affair
  1.   Margaret, Princess of Great Britain, 1930–
2.   Snowdon, Antony Armstrong-Jones, 1st Earl of,
1930– 3.   Windsor, House of 4.   Great Britain—
Princes and princesses—Biography. I. Kahn, Gary,
joint author. II. Title.
DA585.A5M338   941.085′092′2   [B]   77-83854
ISBN 0-8467-0389-0

Text design by Celie Fitzgerald
Production by Planned Production
Manufactured in the United States of America

Two Continents
30 East 42nd Street
New York, New York 10017
      and
Bunch Books
14 Rathbone Place
London W1 England

CONTENTS

THE AUTHORS

ROGER HUTCHINSON, 28, comes from Lancashire and is a professional journalist. He has at various times edited the radical Yorkshire-based fortnightly *Styng*, the underground publications *Oz* and *International Times* and the London entertainments weekly *Time Out*. He has co-authored two books, *The Wisdom of Bruce Lee* and *Man-Eating Sharks*, and is now researching a book on the professional tennis circuit. His work includes writings on politics, football, drug addiction, pornography and travel.

GARY KAHN, 31, comes from the East End of London. He is a professional journalist working for glossy magazines and specialising in candid profiles of the famous. Whilst an undergraduate at Oxford University he edited the University magazine *Isis*. He has worked extensively in London theatre both as a playwright and as a producer. Projects include arts features for the BBC, co-founding an avant garde theatre company *The Almost Free Theatre* in London, children's theatre workshop, a spell running the Drury Lane *Arts Lab* and more recently writing and directing a topical late night revue *Here is the News*.

AUTHORS' PREFACE

There has never been any shortage of biographies, documentaries, and coffee-table books about the Royal House of Windsor. In 1977, Jubilee Year, nearly forty books dealing with the Queen of England and her family were planned in Britain alone. Public interest in the affairs of Royalty, international fascination with the glittering, romantic facade presented to the world by the British Royal Family is as high, perhaps higher, in the supposedly disenchanted 1970's as it has ever been.

But despite this immense acreage of print, and regardless of the hundreds of claims by publishers and authors that their work presents "the true face," "the reality behind the glamour," or "the human story" of Queen Elizabeth II and her family, the private lives and ordinary foibles of this select group of individuals has remained a diligently shrouded mystery.

The reasons for this are not difficult to understand, nor is it the purpose of this book to debate them here. The Royal Family of England has long since recognised the importance of maintaining as much secrecy as is constitutionally possible about its private affairs. A century ago the political theorist Walter Bagehot wrote: "Above all things our royalty is to be reverenced, and if you begin to poke about it you cannot reverence it . . . Its mystery is its life. We must not let in daylight upon the magic."

If anything, the amount of daylight let in upon the private lives of royalty has decreased since Bagehot wrote *The English Constitution* in 1867. In view of the apparently increased accessibility of the modern monarchy, this may seem to be surprising. But the carefully orchestrated public appearances, bland television coverage, sycophantic books, and repetitive magazine articles almost without exception contrive to present to the public an image of members of the Royal Family which is so relentlessly one-dimensional as to be manifestly untrue. A blanket of secrecy has been all the while wrapped tightly around any personal weaknesses or human flaws to which members of the House of Windsor, being flesh and blood, are as prone as the rest of us.

When these flaws and weaknesses do find their way into the public eye, the credibility of the Royal Family is considered to be seriously dented. The abdication of Edward VIII over his desire to marry the twice-divorced Mrs. Wallis Simpson in 1936 so disturbed the Royal Family that even in 1973 Prince William of Gloucester—then 9th in succession to the throne—could say: "One of the reasons why I have never married is that I could not possibly afford to make a mistake and marry the wrong girl. Divorce is an unmentionable subject in our family. I could not make a mistake like Uncle David (Edward VIII)."

Obviously, then, the demands made upon members of the family are severe. They must possess a strong sense of duty, conducting themselves with decorum and dignity at all times. Fortunately, most of the prominent members of the House of Windsor display these qualities in abundance. The Queen, particularly, has in her 25 years on the throne attracted almost universal praise for her calmness and diligence in maintaining the prestige of the crown. She has seen the British monarchy grow stronger during a period of considerable social change. It would be difficult to imagine a more suitable person to stabilise the throne of England.

Her husband, Prince Philip, having no constitutionally defined role was set a difficult task when in 1952 Elizabeth came to the throne. As consort to his wife, metaphorically obliged to walk two paces behind her on all public appearances, he could neither assert himself easily without detriment to Elizabeth, nor could he allow himself to appear as a speechless nonentity. He has cleverly trod the line between the two. Frequently outspoken, his raffish personality, extrovert opinions, and oft-quoted quips have endeared him to the majority of Elizabeth's subjects.

Only their two eldest children have so far been exposed to the full glare of international public attention. Prince Charles and Princess Anne have each managed to grow out of their unusually celebrated childhoods, and have successfully established themselves as adults whose activities the public respects and takes interest in. Anne's brusque lack of manners has on occasion irritated both the press and the public, but the future king, Charles, has acquired over the last few years a confidence and breeziness of manner which certainly pleases his parents. The four of them, together with the ever-radiant Queen Mother, carry together the responsibility of maintaining the salubrious good name which the House of Windsor has so studiously cultivated.

Princess Margaret, the Queen's sister, was never presented with a prescribed role to play. Nor has she—unlike other of her relatives—been able successfully to create one. Margaret's was not an easy upbringing; as the future Queen of England's younger sister she was brought up in a shadow. Perhaps another woman could have found it in herself to overcome the disheartening effects of playing second fiddle or worse for the rest of her life. Perhaps somebody else might have outgrown the depressing experience of being "Margaret of *Nothing*" while her sister became Queen. Perhaps . . . but Margaret was not that other person.

Not that the authorities were to make things easy for her, or attempted to understand her peculiar, vulnerable temperament. By the end of the 1950's she had been denied marriage to the only man she had ever loved because of her supposed responsibilities to an institution—the monarchy—which in its turn had no intention of crediting her with the ability to exercise any responsibility at all. She was expected, it seemed, to live out the rest of her life in a house of great comfort on a massive income, quietly married to somebody approved by the church, the government, and her family—and doing nothing that might offend the proprieties of any of these.

To some young women, this might seem to be a not unattractive prospect. To Margaret, approaching the age of 30, the idea was tedious and she gradually rebelled against it. Throughout the 1960's it became increasingly obvious that Margaret had no great interest in the "Royal business," and no particular intention of finding for herself a suitable role. She started living in a way that no *woman* so close to the reigning monarch had ever done before. It became apparent that this was a reluctant princess, a woman who was more attracted to the newfound social and sexual freedoms of a changing age than to the demands of life as a prominent member of the Royal Family. The chasm between her and her closest relatives was irrevocably revealed when in the 1970's she took as her constant companion a man 17 years her junior, and publicly separated from her husband—the one person whom the Royal Family had once considered might reconcile her wayward lifestyle with the strictures of being 5th in line to the throne of England.

The House of Windsor will survive the unfavourable publicity that it suffered during the breakup of Princess Margaret's marriage—just as it survived the more serious crisis surrounding Edward VIII and Wallis Simpson. Elizabeth II's reign is resilient enough to withstand such unwelcome attentions to the private life of her sister. Margaret, in her turn, will also survive the controversy, returning to her round of royal functions interspersed with lengthy holidays. What has emerged from the whole unfortunate affair is a harsh reminder of the uncompromising discipline required of a member of a *successful* 20th century monarchy, and the fact that without this disciplined code of royal behaviour the life of Princess Margaret would, in all probability, have been a happier one.

RH & GK
London 1977

A FAMILY AFFAIR

1

THE ROYAL FAMILY AND SCANDAL

On Friday, 19 March 1976, a Buckingham Palace spokesman announced that the sixteen-year marriage of Princess Margaret to the Earl of Snowdon was over. The news did not come as a great surprise. For at least a decade friction between the couple had been ill-concealed despite intensive pressure to keep it covered up. As sister of Queen Elizabeth II and fifth in succession to the throne of England, Princess Margaret was expected to maintain the image, if not the reality, of a responsible member of the most respected Royal Family in the world. This she had most flagrantly failed to do. The forty-six-year-old Princess' romantic involvement with twenty-eight-year-old Roddy Llewellyn had been the last straw.

It was widely known that previous sexual infidelities by both Princess Margaret and Lord Snowdon had brought the couple close to parting on a number of occasions. But the need to preserve appearances in order to contradict the persistent and well-founded gossip about their social and sexual goings-on was impressed upon them. At a formal meeting at Buckingham Palace on 18 December 1967, at the time of Snowdon's relationship with Pamela Colin (the present Lady Harlech) the Queen had said

1

to a tearful Margaret, "Why don't each of you go your own way—but please be quiet about it."

The necessity to "be quiet about it" is due to the vulnerable position of the British Royal Family. As "rulers" of a constitutional monarchy, with all the trappings and pomp of a once great Empire, the Royal Family performs only a symbolic function in the governing of the United Kingdom. But as titular head of state the Queen and her family are of inestimable value as figurehead and focus for all that is best and most venerable in Britain. Anything that tarnishes the image of the Royal Family threatens this function and must be avoided at all costs. The Queen is also head of the Church of England and as such stands firmly behind its moral code to which the great majority of her people, permissive society or not, continue to pay lip-service. One of the great achievements of the Royal Family over the last half-century has been to make itself—an aristocratic house of German origins—the bastion, repository and custodian of everything that the average British middle-class person holds most sacred.

The inviolability of the family and the confinement of sex to marriage are pre-eminent in this code. That the Queen, her husband, and her children subscribe to these values is a source of constant delight to millions of her subjects. They are glamorous but they are respectable. Indeed, in 1976, before the break-up of Margaret and Snowdon's marriage, the Royal Family might be said to have chalked up a quite extraordinarily high performance record. In spite of the break-up of the British Empire, and the diminishing political and economic prestige of Great Britain among world powers, the Royal Family was enormously popular. The Queen celebrated her fiftieth birthday in April 1976 to universal accolades; Prince Charles was firmly launched on his career as a naval officer and Princess Anne had just married a fellow horseman, Captain Mark Phillips, in a glittering occasion at Westminster Abbey.

The Royal Family has worked hard for its present high level of popularity. It is served by an extremely capable body of men and women who act as both buffers and weather vanes between the institution and the British public. If the monarchy was to survive it had to change with the times, as indeed it has done. This

2

was achieved by making the Royal Family seem less removed from the lives of the great majority of the British people without losing the essential aura of Royalty. A social function like the presentation of debutantes to the Queen was scrapped, Prince Charles and Princess Anne were sent away to ordinary, if expensive, schools instead of being educated at home, and the Queen and Prince Philip went often on "walkabouts."

Probably the most successful piece of public relations in the last decade was the 110-minute TV film called "The Royal Family." Shown at Christmas 1969, the film follows the Queen and her family going about their business in an unfussy, often humorous way. As the Queen and her husband entered their middle age, they permitted the country to see them doing such ordinary things as going out shopping or having a barbecue as well as good-naturedly receiving one ambassador after another or suffering endless state banquets.

Attention was focused on the emerging and engaging characters of Prince Charles and Princess Anne, who were clearly going to be able to satisfy the public's appetite for glamour and youth, which their parents no longer possessed.

The country was very grateful and the Royal Family's already good reputation was consolidated. One member of it did, however, reflect at the time: "God's tooth, what a narrow squeak Margaret wasn't the eldest daughter. That would have been a disaster. How long would it have lasted if Snowdon had been consort? Dreadful, dreadful."

If the majority of the British public rely on and welcome the continuity of the British Royal Family, that is a measure of how successfully the Royal Family has itself been stage-managed. The monarchy has become synonymous with stability, goodness, honesty and devotion to duty. But this has not always been so. The inability of Princess Margaret and Lord Snowdon to "keep quiet" about their differences reminded the Royal Family of its troubles in the past.

The popular image of the present Queen's great-great grandmother Queen Victoria as a loved and revered old lady representing all that was finest in the great days of the British Empire is almost entirely false. The monarchy was by no means as hedged in by middle-class sentimentality as it is now. Republicanism was rife throughout Europe in the nineteenth century. When Victoria came to the throne in 1837, the memory of the dissolute George IV was still fresh in the minds of most Englishmen and Victoria's marriage to the German Albert of Saxe-Coburg-Gotha, a dour humourless man, did not endear her to her people. After his early death her morbid devotion to his memory resulted in her withdrawal from all public activities to such an extent as to invoke even more hostility, especially in view of the very considerable amounts of public money she continued to receive for services she was unwilling to perform. She was a narrow-minded, crabbed, miserly woman who hated life and treated other people, especially her eldest son Edward, accordingly.

During Prince Albert's lifetime, Queen Victoria had fallen totally under his control. His high-minded, life-denying, puritan principles she retained throughout her life, and attempted to instill them in her children. Queen Victoria's total inability to feel or show any understanding or affection for her children had resulted in their being brought up in the most stilted and isolated circumstances. This was most particularly true of Edward. Her almost pathological hatred and fear of sexuality meant that any normal expression in Edward was rigidly suppressed.

Throughout his adolescence Edward was forever being criticised and found wanting by the Queen who would hold Albert before him as the image of perfection. Edward's upbringing was concerned solely with producing a model prince, as conceived by his parents, who by emulating their rigid system of middle-class virtues would ensure the stability and well-being of the monarchy.

Despite his parents' constant blandishments and their attempts to get him safely married as quickly as possible, Edward managed his first taste of forbidden fruit during the summer of 1861. When he was eighteen he was sent to Curragh in Ireland for a series of pointless military exercises. Edward was delighted when some of his fellow guardsmen at Curragh smuggled into his rooms a pretty young 'actress' called Nellie Clifden, with whom he embarked on the first of his many sexual liaisons. Three months later news of the affair reached the Palace, and there was

4

hell to pay. Albert told his son: "You must not, you dare not be lost. The consequences for the country, for the world, would be too dreadful."

Plans were swiftly made to send Edward on a tour of the Near East. On November 25, Albert went up to see his son at Cambridge where Edward was continuing his affair with Nellie. It was on this visit that Albert caught a chill. Two weeks later he was ill from typhoid fever and died on 14 December 1861. Victoria never forgave or forgot the role that Edward had played in the death of her beloved husband.

The widowed Victoria then entered into a period of mourning that lasted the remaining forty years of her life. While continuing to draw her substantial income from the Civil List, she refused to fulfill even the most minor duties of a constitutional monarch and incurred considerable public hostility as a result. Newspapers and gossip-mongers pounced on the more ridiculous aspects of her life; in particular, her peculiar attachment to her Scots *gillie* (or house-servant), John Brown, who followed her everywhere, much to the consternation of what little remained of the court. By 1869, Edward himself was sufficiently worried by his mother to gently reprimand her: "We live in radical times and the more *the people see the sovereign*, the better it is for the *people* and the *country*."

His advice was not taken. Nor had the Queen, since Albert's death, shared even the smallest part of the constitutional role with her son. Instead he had been put under the charge of the ageing General Sir William Knollys and treated like a schoolboy. Earlier in the decade, showing no regard at all for Edward's feelings in the matter, Victoria had gone ahead with negotiations for her son to marry Princess Alexandra of Denmark. Alexandra was pretty and slightly deaf. She was said to be mild mannered, lacking in opinions, and at eighteen still remarkably childlike. In other words, someone who was dynastically suitable, and sufficiently malleable for Victoria to dominate.

Edward, in disgrace after his affair with the actress, fell in with his mother's plans and proposed. He was accepted by Alexandra in the summer of 1862. The British public received the news with considerable pleasure, only slightly soured by Victoria's simultaneous announcement that the wedding would not take place in London ("she felt incapable of facing the crowds") but in St. George's Chapel at Windsor where no royal wedding had taken place since 1122. Alexandra's arrival in England for the service was warmly welcomed by a nation which since Albert's death had seen precious little of its royal family.

After his marriage, Edward moved into Marlborough House in London and was voted an income of £40,000 a year, plus £10,000 for Alexandra's own use. Together with capital investments and rents from Sandringham this brought Edward's income up to £115,000 a year.

The sum was not excessive in that he was expected to assume the social responsibilities properly belonging to the Crown and which, if he had been king, would be paid for out of Crown incomes. Furthermore, Edward would be taking his place among members of an aristocracy who in many cases had incomes far in excess of his own. Reports that he was spending more than his annual income led to speculation that he must be in debt, a persistent rumour which when linked to his lifelong addiction to gambling was to be a source of great embarrassment to him.

Installed at Marlborough House, married and financially secure enough for the first time to be beyond the immediate supervision of his mother, Edward entered the extraordinary period of his life that lasted nearly forty years. Although heir apparent he was to be denied any real power or influence in political matters at all. As Victoria became increasingly a recluse, Edward's gregarious nature sought out ways to express itself. Despite the five children that Alexandra bore him between 1864 and 1869 the Prince of Wales did not confine his pleasures to those of a family man. Associating with a more informal "fast" set than before his marriage, that included rich Americans, millionaire English Jews and other self-made men from the world of commerce, Edward linked himself to representatives of a vigorous new capitalist class in society. This proved shocking to both the dull conservative aristocracy whose landed interests were already in decline and the emerging mass of the middle class. Edward had embarked on a life of pleasure-seeking that would frequently bring the taint of scandal dangerously close to the monarchy.

Edward's life-long devotion to good living, to beautiful women and gambling meant that he only very slowly enamoured himself to the vast majority of Englishmen. Edward was sixty when he reached the throne and had mellowed considerably by then. Had Victoria died earlier Edward's reckless behaviour might have provoked an enormous amount of trouble for him as king. As it was, only five years after his marriage Edward began to be publicly attacked for activities and associations considered improper to a Prince of Wales.

In February 1867, for example, there was a tremendous furor over his having taken part in a fox-hunt at Badminton on Ash Wednesday. This was a minor fuss, however, compared with the accounts of his exploits in Paris shortly after. Ostensibly, Edward had gone to Paris to open the British section of the Great Exhibition. But in the notorious company of the Ducs de Grammont-Caderousse and de Mouchy, Edward was introduced to some of Europe's most exotic and expensive courtesans. Cora Pearl, for example, had herself served up naked on a silver platter at the Café des Anglais for the Prince's pleasure. Guilia Beneni, who rejoiced in the title "the biggest sinner in Paris," arrived at the Maison d'Or in a diaphanous dress which when asked to show the Prince her best side, she flipped up to reveal her shapely buttocks.

Edward conducted a not altogether discreet affair with the actress Hortense Sneider, and gossip of his gambling also began to appear in the English papers. Victoria vainly attempted to get Edward to moderate his behaviour. "So long as the nation has confidence in the character of the sovereign the throne of this empire may be regarded as secure," she wrote to him.

A racing scandal the following year over the financial ruin and early death of one of Edward's close friends, Lord Hastings, induced an all-out assault by the press on "certain" sections of the privileged classes. *The Times* wrote: "When a peer of high rank drags his dignity in the dirt he stains his order."

In 1870 Edward was for the first time exposed personally to public outrage when he appeared in court at the Mordaunt divorce case. Sir Charles Mordaunt M.P. had filed a petition of divorce against his young wife, Harriet, citing two of the Prince's constant companions, Lord Cole and Sir Frederick Johnstone, as co-respondents. After she had given birth to a blind baby and believing the cause the venereal disease carried by Sir Frederick Johnstone, Lady Harriet had confessed to her husband that he was not the father of the child and that she had been intimate with Johnstone, Cole, the Prince of Wales and "others, often and in open day." Sir Charles had then forced open his wife's desk and discovered a valentine and a handkerchief and letters from the Prince and other men.

Although he was not subjected to cross-examination, Edward was obliged to take the stand where he firmly denied that any adultery had taken place. Great care was taken that Edward's letters were not read out in open court. Sir Charles' suit was in the end rejected on the grounds of his wife's evident insanity at the time of her confession. Ever since the birth of the blind child she had been quite deranged, continually smearing herself with excrement, and threatening both her own and her child's life.

Although Edward had not even been accused of adultery, much damage had been done to his reputation. *Reynold's Newspaper* wrote: "If the Prince of Wales is an accomplice in bringing dishonour to the homestead of an English gentleman; if he has assisted in rendering an honourable man miserable for life; if unbridled sensuality and lust have led him to violate the laws of honour and hospitality—then such a man, placed in the position he is, should not only be expelled from decent society, but is utterly unfit and unworthy to rule over this country, or even sit on its legislature."

Attempts were made to quell the scandal by having Edward make a great show of appearing in public as frequently as possible in the company of his wife. Alexandra, a simple and forgiving soul, was to remain extremely popular with the British public throughout her life and her constant demonstrations of loyalty to her erring husband were of enormous benefit to Edward in his all-too-frequent falls from grace.

In 1871, with the collapse of the French Empire and the groundswell of republicanism in England reaching its height, the monarchy was in as precarious a position as it had been for half a century. The public was incensed again and again by Edward's gambling. As one newspaper put it, he was staking gold "upon the chance of a card or the roll of a ball—gold, be it remembered, that he obtains from the toil and sweat of English working men, without himself producing the value of a half-penny." Victoria's continuing seclusion was also attacked as further proof of the uselessness of monarchy.

By the end of that year, however, the more serious aspects of this anti-monarchist climate had abated. In the first place, the gruesome events of the Paris Commune dampened the fervour of republican sympathisers, and secondly, Edward fell seriously ill in November, supposedly of typhoid fever. There is nothing, not even a marriage or a coronation, to rally the British innate devotion to the monarchy as much as a royal illness does. Edward duly got worse, and the crowds gathered outside the Palace anxiously waiting for bulletins from his doctors. The republican politician Sir Charles Dilke found himself shouted down at public meetings by crowds singing "Rule Britannia" and the national anthem.

On December 18, the doctors announced Edward to be out of danger. There was general rejoicing throughout England. Dr. Gull, who had brought Edward through his ordeal, was given a baronetcy, and plans were laid for a formal day of public thanksgiving. Held at St. Paul's Cathedral, it was attended by 13,000 people. Even Victoria agreed to take part. Both for the Prince and for the Crown the thanksgiving service was a great triumph.

In spite of Prime Minister Gladstone's arguments, Victoria continued to deny Edward a political apprenticeship, and he returned to his old way of life after his recovery. If he had learned anything from the Mordaunt divorce case it was to leave young newly-married women alone. Otherwise he continued his rounds of pleasure. In 1873, Edward's newly appointed private secretary Francis Knollys wrote to Lord Roseberry requesting him to place his London house at the disposal of the Prince for entertaining his "actress friends." Among these were Sarah Bernhardt, Lily Langtry, Lady Brooke, (later Lady Warwick) Miss Chamberlayne (the vivacious daughter of an American millionaire), the Hon. Mrs. George Keppel and Mrs. Agnes Keyser. As

9

a popular saying of the time had it, "He preferred men to books and women to either!"

After 1874, Edward resumed his visits to Paris, often incognito. He established liaisons with the Comtesse Edmonde de Portales, the greatest of the French beauties to attract him; the Baronne Alphonse de Rothschild, whose receptions at the Faubourg St. Honoré have become legendary; and the Princesse de Sagan, wife of the great-nephew of Talleyrand. Other beauties with less exalted names entertained him when he stayed at the less prestigious Hotel Bristol or dined at the still notorious Café des Anglais.

In 1875, there was a rancorous debate in the House of Commons over the £100,000 granted to Edward for his forthcoming trip to India. It was brought out that during his visit he would be receiving presents valued at at least £200,000 which would become his personal property. Then a worse scandal erupted.

One of Edward's close friends, forty-five-year-old Colonel Valentine Baker, commander of the Prince's own regiment, was charged in June with the attempted rape of Miss Rebecca Kate Dickenson in a first class railway carriage travelling between Petersfield and Clapham. After a sensational court case with much talk of "vile passions," Baker was found guilty of indecent assault. Rape had only been averted, the court declared, by Miss Dickenson opening the train carriage door and climbing out on to the footboard, "determined to perish rather than re-enter."

Baker was sentenced to twelve months and a £500 fine, but revelation of animal passions running riot among the ruling classes made Edward's loose and easy manners a focus for much public anger, and special security measures had to be taken to protect Edward as one aftermath of the trial.

No sooner was Edward in India than another sexual scandal arose that implicated him more seriously. It concerned the planned elopement of Lady Aylesford, wife of Lord Aylesford, one of Edward's companions in India, with Lord Blandford, elder son of the Duke of Marlborough and brother of Randolph Churchill, M.P. To prevent her husband from divorcing her on the grounds of her adultery with Blandford, Lady Aylesford had given Blandford some letters written to her by Edward some years earlier. Blandford gave these letters to Churchill, who threatened to make the contents of the letters public unless Edward persuaded Aylesford not to seek a divorce. (Churchill showed the letters to Alexandra, telling her that were they printed they "would ensure that Edward would never occupy the throne of England".) Edward furiously cabled Churchill challenging him to a duel. He replied that Edward knew perfectly well a duel could not take place between a Prince and his subject.

Eventually some order was restored by Disraeli, who managed to dissuade Aylesford from going to court and prevailed upon the Blandford faction to keep quiet. It was eight years, however, before Edward forgave Randolph Churchill for so nearly causing a public scandal. And eight years was a long time, in view of Edward's continued fascination with Churchill's beautiful American wife Jennie.

During the 1880's, Edward seemed to have learned something from these near-scrapes and attempted to act a little more discreetly. He undertook some quite successful royal visits abroad, and Alexandra was steadfastly loyal. She did, however, have a passionate admirer, the Hon. Oliver Montague, who was constantly at her side and made little attempt to conceal his devotion. Alexandra did not reject his attentions, and it soon became accepted that her first waltz after supper was reserved for him. His death in 1893 was a great blow for her.

A subject of much more concern to Edward was the increasingly dissolute behaviour of his eldest son Albert Victor, born in 1864, who proved impossible to educate and had developed a taste for only the most corrupt of amusements. An attempt to inculcate Albert Victor with some sense of responsibility by making him join his younger brother George (later George V) in the navy proved of little benefit. In fact, the wild influence of his elder brother resulted in George committing what was perhaps the greatest indiscretion of his life.

After an ill-fated infatuation in 1883 with a Roman Catholic commoner called Julie Stonor, George had been stationed in Malta. There he met and according to a rumour that was to persist well into the following century actually *married* an admiral's daughter, a Miss Culme-Seymour. The affair (or marriage) of Edward's second son was hushed up with great speed and expense.

Albert Victor's behaviour was too far gone for any such course of action to be sustained for long. By the end of the 1880's his activities in the company of his fellow officers were becoming so debauched that he was in great danger of being arrested. A police raid discovered him in a notorious homosexual brothel off the Tottenham Court Road. He was showing signs of insanity and was almost certainly suffering from syphilis. The possibility that Albert Victor, Duke of Clarence, was in fact responsible for the host of gruesome murders of London prostitutes attributed to Jack the Ripper remains quite open. It is clear that some degree of high-powered pressure was used to prevent the police from catching the murderer, and it remains a troubling fact that after Albert Victor's early death in 1892, no more Jack the Ripper murders were committed.

Edward attempted to take the one course of action on Albert Victor's behalf which might make him half-way respectable: to get him married. In 1890, Albert Victor agreed, but said the girl he wanted was the wholly unsuitable Princess Hélène d'Orleans, daughter of the Pretender to the French throne, who in addition to everything else was of course a Roman Catholic. Albert Victor was persuaded to change the object of his affections and in December 1891, proposed to and was accepted by Princess May of Teck. It is doubtful that Princess May had much idea of the character of the man she was engaged to, but fortunately she never had a chance to find out. In January 1892, Albert Victor, aged twenty-eight, contracted a new virus called Russian Flu. Combined with a weak constitution undermined by his continual indulgences and dissipations, it killed him on January 14.

Princess May was not, however, lost to England. In the spring of the following year she got engaged to brother George. As Queen Mary after George V's accession, she came to embody all those respectable and dignified virtues which the British so love to see in their monarchs. Albert Victor's death had saved her from a fate probably several times worse than death and the

Edward VII's dissolute and uncontrollable eldest son, Albert Victor the Duke of Clarence. Was this the face of Jack the Ripper?

country from the possibility of the throne being occupied by a man with the morals of a guttersnipe and as much inclination to be a constitutional monarch as Caligula or Nero.

Edward's maturer years were not, however, without incident. In 1891, he had been up to his old tricks again and once more found himself in the tangles of a public scandal. That summer he was called upon to give evidence in a case involving alleged cheating at baccarat during a gambling party at Tranby Croft. The revelations were extremely unpleasant. On the opening day of Ascot, Edward was greeted with hisses and boos. Even *The New York Times* commented: "The scandal cannot fail to add to the growing conviction that royalty is a burden to the British taxpayer." It went on to seriously doubt whether the monarchy would survive the death of the Queen.

A second crisis for Edward in 1891 arose when the wife of one of his close friends, Lord Beresford, intercepted a letter from the beautiful Lady Brooke which made it quite clear that Beresford had been having an affair with her. Lady Brooke approached the Prince of Wales, who was not impervious to her charms, and requested that he recover the letter for her. Edward twice visited Lady Beresford and asked her to return the letter. She refused. Edward was furious and ensured that she was ostracised by London society.

Edward was now seen regularly with Lady Brooke. Lord Beresford, who had been abroad, returned to find his mistress stolen and his wife a social outcast. He demanded that Edward reinstate his wife, otherwise he would reveal details of the Prince's private life to the press. As in the Aylesford affair, Edward found himself in a difficult position. He had no option but to make a formal apology to Lady Beresford, now fully reconciled with her husband, assuring her that "he had never intended to cause her any inconvenience." Edward never forgave Lord Beresford.

Lady Brooke continued to be Edward's principal mistress, usurping Lily Langtry. Unlike her predecessor, however, she was never received by Alexandra at Marlborough House, and the affair with Edward, who greatly admired her beauty, ended shortly after her conversion to socialism, an ideology he found intolerable.

14

Edward in 1897 at a fancy dress ball: an elderly Prince of Wales with too much time on his hands

In general, Edward was able to conduct himself with more decorum as he got older and was gratified to find himself less frequently under attack. But he was amazed by the outburst of cheering when his horse Persimmon won the Derby in 1896. The British can forgive a winning sportsman almost anything.

By 1900, after a number of successes on the turf, Edward had become a truly popular figure. His personal life had become remarkably tranquil, attributable to two remarkable women who became his mistresses in 1898. The first was Alice Keppel, wife of Sir George Keppel and the woman who became the last great love of his life; it says a great deal for Alexandra's generous nature that at the end of Edward's life she sent for Mrs. Keppel to come to his deathbed to say goodbye. The second was Agnes Keyser, a forty-six-year-old trained nurse and daughter of an extremely wealthy stockbroker, who gave Edward the kind of solicitude and comfort that he valued increasingly as he entered his sixties.

When Victoria died in January 1901, Edward assumed the throne confident that in spite of earlier scandals he would be welcomed by most of his subjects. His coronation in August of the following year was the occasion of an immense effusion of loyalty and patriotism, rendered all the more poignant by its two-month postponement on account of the King's grave illness.

Edward's nine-year reign restored the monarchy to the people. He was a lovable, recognisable human being whose foibles the nation had grown to love. A political and social conservative, he was nevertheless keenly aware that his authority depended on the tolerance of his subjects. This understanding stood him in good stead and taught him the value of compromise, wisdom he passed on to his son George.

In a Britain which was no longer indisputably the richest and most powerful country in the world, there was much to be said for a head of state who was fully conscious of the value of pomp and drama in public life. Edward's public appearances as King were rapturously received and he brought to his role as monarch a style, dash and authority that were totally to elude his successor.

George V succeeded his father in 1910, and was, by contrast, extremely dull. Yet this very dullness worked in the interests of the monarchy. George had never forgotten the dissolute example of his brother Albert Victor; together with his wife Mary, a ram-rod of moral rectitude, George V became an exemplar of middle class domesticity. George V was the first English king to outwardly and in fact conform to the standards of conduct of the overwhelming majority of his people.

Hard-working and punctilious, George V, who reigned for twenty-six years, could claim the remarkable achievement of making his subjects feel *grateful* for the job they were paying their king to do.

The royal family was a natural focus for patriotic sentiment during the First World War and it was decided to change its name from "Saxe-Coburg-Gotha" to "Windsor." George had also agreed not to drink while the war was on, on the advice of Prime Minister Lloyd George. Since it was well known that the king was a heavy drinker, this was a prodigious response to the call of duty. He abstained, but he bore a grudge against Lloyd George for the rest of his life.

In fact, the only "scandal" of George V's reign was the way his children were brought up. Convinced that it was correct for children to fear their parents, he kept himself remote from them at all times. Queen Mary had an almost pathological disgust for children and paid little attention to them. The two eldest boys, Edward (later Edward VIII) and Albert (later George VI) were brought up by a strict and sadistic nanny who made certain this distance was maintained. When she took Prince Edward into the drawing room to see the King and Queen, for example, she would surreptitiously pinch or twist his arm so that he screamed and was quickly returned to her. Her attempts to break Albert's left-handedness resulted in a stammer that handicapped him for much of his life.

As his children grew up, George V became more authoritative. "I was always frightened of *my* father; they must be frightened of me," he remarked.

His attitude reflected his insecurity, and combined with an

inflated belief in the dignity befitting a monarch meant that his behaviour with them was frequently harsh and distant. Like Queen Victoria, he was forever finding fault.

Following the traditional pattern, the children were educated at home. Their tutor, a Mr. Hansell, was woefully inadequate. Princes Edward and Albert were then sent to the naval college at Osborne which had a rigid code of conduct that prevented any informality between them and their fellow cadets.

When Edward then went up to Oxford, arrangements were made where he should live, how he should attend lectures and so on, which meant that he was totally cut off from normal university life. His father regularly wrote him about duties as Prince of Wales.

The actual ceremony of Edward's Investiture as Prince of Wales at Caernarvon was dreamed up by Lloyd George as a piece of mediaeval tomfoolery to boost royal prestige and as such was deeply resented by Edward. During the First World War he constantly asked to be sent to the Front: "What does it matter if I am killed? I have four brothers."

In March 1918, he met Mrs. Freda Dudley Ward, then wife of a Liberal M.P., at a party in Belgrave Square and almost immediately fell madly and abjectly in love with her. From 1919 to 1934, Edward's life practically revolved around Mrs. Freda Dudley Ward. In London, he would call on her every day at five o'clock, staying with her the whole evening, or if this was impossible, going away only to return to her house later that same night. Wherever she went for a summer holiday he would take a house in the same area.

George V and Queen Mary were greatly alarmed by their son's liaison with Mrs. Dudley Ward but were unable to break the hold that she had over him. After his immensely successful trips to Canada and the U.S.A., to New Zealand and Australia and to India, Edward—by now universally dubbed "Prince Charming" on account of his dashing good looks—would always return to the arms of Freda. When brother Albert married Elizabeth Bowes-Lyon in 1923, he received a congratulatory letter from the King: "You have always been so sensible and easy to work with. And you have always been ready to listen to any advice

18

and to agree with my opinions about people and things, that I feel we have always got on well together (very different from dear Edward)".

In the years after the war, society underwent a number of radical changes. The jazz age, with its night clubs and cocktail bars, was looked upon with horror by George V. However much his father disliked the new fashion, he could not prevent Edward from luxuriating in the heady alternatives to the stuffy formality of court functions. In 1924, Mrs. Dudley Ward became legally separated from her husband. Edward repeatedly asked her to "go away with him," but it became clear that she regarded him as not a totally successful lover and did not return his love with the same intensity.

By 1924, Edward was having a number of short affairs with other women, most notably with Lady Furness, although he continued seeing Freda Dudley Ward regularly. These women had one thing in common: they were all married.

Ironically, it was Lady Furness who in the winter of 1930 first introduced Edward to a fellow American, Mrs. Wallis Simpson. Currently married to Ernest Simpson, an American lawyer based in London, Wallis Simpson had been divórced in December 1927 from Winfield Spencer, a U.S. naval officer. She was almost exactly two years younger than the Prince of Wales, but had seen a good deal of the world. She was an extremely forceful and outgoing woman and Edward was immediately attracted to her.

In early 1932, Edward started to invite Mrs. Simpson—together with Ernest Simpson—to spend weekends at his Fort Belvedere retreat near Windsor. During the following year Edward paid visits to her at her London flat, which Ernest conveniently vacated for him. Then between January and March 1934, Lady Furness paid a visit to America where her affair with Prince Aly Khan destroyed any feelings Edward still had for her. The field was wide open for Wallis Simpson.

In May 1934, Mrs. Freda Dudley Ward telephoned the Prince of Wales who for the first time in seventeen years had allowed more than a week to go by without either visiting or telephoning her. She was startled to be told by Edward's telephonist, "I have something so terrible to tell you. I have orders not to put you through." Mrs. Dudley Ward did not, in fact, see Edward again.

By the early summer of 1934, it became apparent that Edward was totally under the spell of Wallis Simpson. In a few weeks there was more gossip and scandal than in the whole of the previous forty years. Previously, Edward's affairs had been kept out of public view. But with Wallis Simpson he began to act with a reckless and even ostentatious abandon. He bought her jewels in ridiculous profusion and would insist—much to the chagrin of friends and advisers—on being *constantly* in her company.

Ernest Simpson found that he had "business commitments" when Edward invited the Simpsons to accompany him to Biarritz in the summer of 1934, and Wallis went alone. In the autumn of that year, Wallis was presented to the King and Queen for the first and last time at the wedding of Edward's brother, the Duke of Kent. For the rest of that year and for the whole of 1935, Edward and Wallis were inseparable.

1935 was the year of George V's Jubilee. The celebration was an enormous success. At the close of the day the King had broadcast a message of thanks to his "very dear people." "I had no idea that I was so popular," he said privately. "I am beginning to think they must really like me for myself."

Yet he was intensely worried about the future. He had no idea of how to talk to his son. The Archbishop of Canterbury, when consulted about the Simpson affair, hoped that Edward might "grow out of it." To Prime Minister Stanley Baldwin, George declared: "After I am dead the boy will ruin himself in twelve months."

George V died on 20 January 1936. On December 10 of that same year, Edward VIII abdicated in order to marry Wallis Simpson in the most notorious blaze of scandal and publicity the monarchy had undergone in half a century. George V's prophesy came true with astonishing accuracy.

Any hopes in royal circles that Edward might adopt a more responsible attitude towards his private life when he became King were immediately disappointed. On the evening following his very first public engagement he dined alone with Mrs. Simpson.

20

(top) George V reviewing the troops in 1935, with his sons behind him. "After I am dead, the boy will ruin himself in twelve months" (bottom left) Under the spell of Mrs. Simpson. Edward and Wallis holidaying alone in Biarritz, summer of 1934 (bottom right) On the post-abdication visit to Nazi Germany, Goebbel's propaganda machine proclaimed the Windsors as "The real King and the real Queen of Great Britain"

Immediate alarm was caused by the casual attitude with which he dealt with royal business. Unlike his father who dutifully submitted to the grind of reading boring state papers and receiving endless officials, Edward was impatient and unwilling to apply himself for any length of time to these tedious tasks.

As a consequence, the red dispatch boxes in which state papers are traditionally delivered to the monarch would often remain lying about at Ford Belvedere for weeks before being returned. The contents of these boxes were frequently highly confidential, and Edward's casual attitude towards them constituted a grave security risk.

Throughout his short reign, Edward was under constant surveillance by worried security chiefs aware of the risks inherent in the King's indiscreet behaviour. Not the least of these fears was linked to the supposed connections between Mrs. Simpson and Nazi Germany. The Nazi ambassador in London, Ribbentrop, had certainly made approaches to her, and as early as July 1935, the German Embassy had attempted to ingratiate itself with the then Prince of Wales by inviting Mrs. Simpson to a grand banquet. What is certain is that Edward as Prince of Wales had led the Nazis to believe that he did not look unfavourably upon their regime. The Nazis themselves, failing to understand the workings of a constitutional monarchy, attached an exaggerated importance to Edward's accession. They believed that Edward's popularity with the masses could be used when he became King to counterbalance anti-Nazi tendencies in British government policy.

The Foreign Office did become increasingly concerned about the marked pro-Nazi sympathies expressed by the new king in 1936, the year in which Germany re-occupied the Rhineland. Ribbentrop went so far as to write to Hitler two years later that "Edward VIII had to abdicate since it was not certain whether because of his views he would co-operate in an anti-German policy of the British Government."

Certainly in 1937, after the abdication and his marriage to Mrs. Simpson, the Duke and Duchess of Windsor, as they then became, undertook a visit to Nazi Germany where they were received by Hitler himself. Nazi wartime plans to reinstate Edward on the throne of England were taken sufficiently seriously for Edward to be whisked out of Europe via Lisbon to take up the singularly ridiculous appointment of "Governor of the Bahamas" for the duration of the war.

But the principal cause for concern upon Edward's accession was quite simply his continued infatuation with Mrs. Simpson. The King of England, head of the British Empire and of the Church of England was having an affair with a married American commoner and doing precious little to conceal the fact. One of Edward's closest advisers, Walter Monckton, began to be seriously alarmed when it dawned on him that Edward might actually be intending to marry Mrs. Simpson, if she were free to do so. Monckton consulted Winston Churchill on the matter, who replied, "The existence of *Mr.* Simpson is a safeguard." Churchill was nevertheless anxious that Monckton "should make it plain to the King how important it was that his friendship with Mrs. Simpson should not be flaunted in the eyes of the public."

In the summer of 1936, Edward, tired of the rebuffs he was receiving from the Establishment, decided to take a Balkan holiday with Mrs. Simpson on a chartered yacht, the *Nahlin*. The cruise was a riot of indiscretion. Everywhere they went he and Mrs. Simpson were photographed together, and his feelings for her were quite undisguised. Edward was defying convention in every conceivable way. Passing through the Corinth Canal he stood on the bridge wearing nothing but shorts and a pair of binoculars while crowds on the banks cheered him, yelling, "Long Live Love."

The English public (unlike the rest of the world) were kept in ignorance of Mrs. Simpson's presence on the *Nahlin*. The *Weekly Illustrated News*, for example, even went so far as to cut Mrs. Simpson out of a photograph that showed her at the King's side before publishing it.

On his return from the cruise Edward continued to be oblivious to anything but his need to be with Wallis. Having reluctantly agreed to spend the customary two weeks at Balmoral with Queen Mary and a collection of Cabinet ministers, bishops and Establishment figures, Edward invited Mrs. Simpson to join him there! This was flagrant enough, but he went still further by personally meeting her at Ballater station on the same day he had refused to open a new hospital in Aberdeen because he was still in mourning for his father. He also insisted that Mrs. Simpson's name be published in the Court Circulars. Only with the greatest difficulty were the rumours about his affair with Wallis Simpson kept out of the British press.

By the beginning of October, Edward had decided to marry Wallis Simpson. She was still married to Ernest Simpson but filed a divorce petition against him which he docilely agreed not to contest. What rewards Ernest Simpson received for his extraordinary amenity throughout the entire affair have never been revealed.

The divorce proceedings would, quite naturally, claim a considerable amount of public attention, but Edward took the unprecedented step on October 16 of summoning to Buckingham Palace Lord Beaverbrook and Esmond Harmsworth, who between them controlled practically the entire British press. This meeting resulted in a "gentlemen's agreement" to keep the divorce off the front pages and the King's association with Wallis Simpson in the dark.

Wallis Simpson obtained her decree *nisi* on October 27. This would then be made absolute on April 27, giving Edward sufficient time to marry her before the coronation scheduled for May 12.

Prime Minister Baldwin realised the implications of the King's desire for the speeding up of the Simpson divorce. He almost certainly had a severe constitutional crisis on his hands. The good name of the monarchy, so carefully built up, would be contaminated by the wishes of the King to marry a woman twice divorced. Cosmo Lang, Archbishop of Canterbury, was perhaps even more appalled at the prospect. Like Baldwin and other leading figures, the Archbishop had been receiving press cuttings, photographs and hostile letters from abroad which attacked the King's behaviour throughout the summer. Like many others he felt "the monarchy was being vulgarised and degraded, that mud was being thrown on sacred things."

On October 20 Baldwin urgently requested to see the King in a desperate attempt to convince him the divorce proceedings must be stopped. But Edward insisted that this was a matter concerning Mrs. Simpson alone. Baldwin attempted to remind Edward of the unique position occupied by the British monarchy and that the prestige of the institution was being threatened by his scandalous behaviour with Mrs. Simpson. He told Edward that "although it is true that standards are lower since the war it only leads people to expect higher standards from their King. People expect more from their King than they did a hundred years ago."

The "gentlemen's agreement" could not be expected to hold up for much longer. At the divorce, two press photographers had their cameras smashed by the police, and reporters were forcibly prevented from following Mrs. Simpson. The foreign press could not be silenced, and on November 13, the King's principal private secretary, Major Alec Hardinge, wrote to the King that it was only a matter of time before the restraint of the British press collapsed. The only way out, he said, was "for Mrs. Simpson to go abroad without further delay . . ."

Edward was furious. But Hardinge was acting quite correctly in reporting to his master the facts as they then stood. In particular, Hardinge had received a number of communications from Lord Tweedsmuir, Governor-General of Canada, and Stanley Bruce, High Commissioner for Australia, which expressed in the strongest possible language the fears throughout the Empire that Edward's behaviour was damaging the prestige of the throne. They expressed universal anathema to the prospect of the King's marriage to Mrs. Simpson.

Baldwin saw Edward at Buckingham Palace on November 16, and for the first time was told by the King that he intended to marry Mrs. Simpson. Baldwin told Edward that the Government and the Dominions would oppose this, to which Edward replied that he was "prepared to go." Edward duly told his family of his decision, much to the shock of Albert, Duke of York, who would succeed him as George VI. Queen Mary's anger and shame at her son's total disregard for the dignity of the crown—so assiduously cultivated by her husband—was to stay with her for the rest of her life.

On November 18 and 19, Edward made a visit to South

Wales where, moved by the terrible poverty he saw, he made his famous comment, "something ought to be done: something will be done." There was a great outburst of public approval and his hopes were raised temporarily that Baldwin might be resisted. This coincided with the suggestion to Mrs. Simpson by Esmond Harmsworth that she might consider a morganatic marriage to Edward. She would be consort, but not Queen. Edward passed on the suggestion to Baldwin who was noncommittal but promised to ask the Cabinet and the Dominions' advice. Without realising it at the time, Edward had trapped himself. Having sought his Prime Minister's advice, he was constitutionally bound to accept it.

While Baldwin collected the ammunition for his next meeting with Edward, the British press' self-censorship finally gave way, and "the King's affair" began to be discussed in print for the first time. The event which precipitated the onslaught was an astonishing outburst on December 1 by the Bishop of Bradford, Dr. Blunt. In an address initiating a "Recall to Religion," planned by the Archbishop of Canterbury to coincide with the coming coronation, Blunt chastised the King for his lack of "self dedication" and reminded him of "the need to do his duty properly—we hope that he is aware of this need. Some of us wish that he gave more positive signs of such self awareness."

The press took up Blunt's attack. Beaverbrook tried to get Edward to lift the restrictions in order to come out openly in *his* newspapers in support of Edward marrying a twice-divorced woman. But Edward did not want to divide the country on the issue or expose Wallis Simpson to the publicity such a campaign would stir up.

On the afternoon of December 2, Baldwin had the Cabinet and the Dominions' rejection of the morganatic marriage proposal in his pocket when he went to see the King. Combined with the attacks upon him in the press this was enough for Edward. The following morning Wallis Simpson left England disguised as "Mrs. Harris" in the company of Lord Brownlow to await further developments in the Cannes villa of her old friends, the Herman Rogers.

On December 4, Edward foolishly and vainly attempted to

26

persuade Baldwin to allow him to appeal to the British people over the heads of the Government. Baldwin pointed out not only the unconstitutional nature of such a course of action but also that it would certainly result in the rejection of Edward's plan to marry Mrs. Simpson while remaining King. A brief attempt was made that evening by a "King's Party," including Churchill and Walter Monckton, and backed by Beaverbrook, to persuade Edward that if he chose to fight Baldwin he could win. Edward was fortified, but only temporarily. The following morning he sent word to Baldwin of his formal intention to abdicate. Beaverbrook commented simply: "Our cock won't fight." (Twenty years later, when asked why he had supported Edward during the Abdication Crisis, Beaverbrook replied equally sharply: "To bugger Baldwin.")

In spite of pleas over the telephone from Cannes by Wallis Simpson to think again, Edward remained resolute. On December 11, the King made his famous Abdication broadcast which had been "read and embellished" by Churchill. In abdicating the throne of England he told his people how he had "found it impossible to carry the heavy burden of responsibility without the help and support of the woman I love." He commended his brother and successor to them: ". . . and he has one matchless blessing enjoyed by so many of you and not bestowed on me— a happy home life with his children . . . And now we all have a new King. God bless you all. God save the King."

George VI, as he now became, was thus suddenly thrust into a role for which he had had little preparation. On the first night of his reign, George confided to Louis Mountbatten (uncle of the future Duke of Edinburgh): "Dickie, this is absolutely terrible. I never wanted this to happen; I'm quite unprepared for it. I've never seen a state paper; I'm only a naval officer; it's the only thing I know about." Mountbatten replied that George V had said exactly the same thing when the Duke of Clarence died.

As Duke of York, he had been a modest family man who only with the greatest difficulty and the aid of his wife had managed to overcome the appalling stammer that afflicted him since childhood. Until 1936, he and his wife had unspectacularly carried out the usual round of royal visits and tours expected of second-ranking royals.

Having constantly been in the shadow of his glamorous elder brother, George had grave doubts about his ability to bring to the throne the aura of majesty and distinction which he felt necessary. In the end, it was his very lack of brilliance, his comfortable domesticity, and his dogged devotion to duty—all so very much like his father—that made him so successful a king.

His happy marriage was much appreciated in 1936. He was devoted to his wife, a charming woman who was to prove extremely adept at cultivating a royal "common touch," be it a smile or a wave, that has endured for over thirty years and remains to delight millions to this day; and had two pretty daughters, Princess Elizabeth, born in 1926, and Princess Margaret, born in 1930.

George VI conferred the title of Duke of Windsor upon his elder brother, together with an income of £25,000 a year, with the understanding that the ex-King was not to return to England without the consent of the King and the Government of the day. Less public were settlements between the brothers over the transferring of the estates of Balmoral and Sandringham that under the wills of Victoria and George V had been left to Edward for life. George probably paid his brother around £1,000,000 and an additional annual income of £60,000 for these. Edward didn't do too badly.

The Duke of Windsor's marriage to Mrs. Simpson was set for June 1937, at the Chateau de Cande in France. It was hardly surprising that there were no representatives of the Royal Family in attendance. What was bitterly unexpected, however, was the arrival of Walter Monckton on the afternoon before the wedding with a letter from George VI stating that the future Duchess of Windsor was to be denied the status and title of Her Royal Highness. For sheer nastiness and vicious timing the letter could hardly have been bettered.

George VI was never to enjoy the best of health. The unlooked-for pressures of kingship took their toll and in the opinion of his family were responsible for his early death. His wife, now Queen Elizabeth, the Queen Mother, has never forgiven the Duke and, more pointedly, the Duchess of Windsor, for this. She, more than any other member of the Royal Family, continued to refuse the formal title of Her Royal Highness to the Duchess. The denial of this title for his beloved wife soured the Duke of Windsor for the rest of his life.

George VI was crowned on his brother's Coronation Day, May 12, 1937, together with Queen Elizabeth. The crown was back on the head of a respectable family man, thank God and Baldwin for that. Not having been trained for the job, George had from the outset to rely heavily on the advice of his prime ministers and household officials, which well suited the increasingly limited influence of the monarchy during this century. Edward VIII would undoubtedly have been more truculent. He would have attempted to assert the political role of the monarch in ways which could have been extremely embarrassing for the Government. The Foreign Office wouldn't have relished the prospect of Goering at Balmoral.

At the outbreak of the Second World War, George VI broadcast to the nation "as if I were able to cross your threshold and speak to you myself." He spoke of the "need to stand firm and united in this time of trial." He was forty-three, his wife thirty-nine, Princess Elizabeth thirteen, and Princess Margaret nine. In the five years of the war, the Royal Family became a focus for patriotic attention and became so inextricably identified with the whole war effort as to become almost revered.

In and out of a succession of uniforms, George, accompanied frequently by his wife and daughters, prettily turned out, would pop up everywhere and bestow a royal sense of occasion upon whomever he happened to be visiting. During the Battle of Britain after two small German bombs happened to fall on Buckingham Palace, Queen Elizabeth could say with a straight face—and presumably without losing her stiff upper lip: "I'm glad we've been bombed. It makes me feel I can look the East End in the face." (They were nowhere near the place at the time.)

George VI's activities during the war were without doubt greatly appreciated by most of the British people. He may not have actually *done* much, but, my goodness, how well he did what he did do. When he was visiting a bombed site in London in

1941, an onlooker had shouted, "Thank God for a good King" to which the King replied, "Thank God for a good people." Not very witty, perhaps, but in heaven's name how worthy!

The entire Royal Family emerged from World War II gilded by the gratitude of a victorious nation. This warm feeling survived the arrival of the Welfare State with the Labour Party's victory in 1945, and the rapid disintegration of the British Empire after the granting of independence to India in 1947. During the period of austerity which followed the peace, the Royal Family was careful not to flaunt its wealth too flagrantly. Newspapers even carried stories about whale meat being served at Buckingham Palace.

The public's appetite for dollops of royal glamour was not neglected either. In 1947, for example, Princess Elizabeth celebrated her twenty-first birthday with a broadcast in which she told the Commonwealth that princesses were human beings too and felt "very much the same on their birthdays as other girls."

Three months later she became engaged to handsome young Lieutenant Philip Mountbatten, and in November they were married at Westminster Abbey. The following year Prince Charles was born and the Silver Wedding of the King and Queen was celebrated in a twenty mile motorcade to St. Paul's. "We were dumbfounded over our reception," wrote George to his mother, presumably not using the royal "we" on this occasion. "It spurs us on to further efforts."

George VI lived only another three years, but by the time of his death in February 1952, he had effectively re-established the monarchy as a stable and popular institution in an era of enormous social change. Without destroying its mystique he had, if anything, added to its prestige by his and his family's dedicated application to his public duties. When Elizabeth heard of the King's death and of her ascension she was, appropriately enough, halfway up a tree in Kenya while on an official tour of Africa.

The new queen was an attractive twenty-five-year-old mother of two (Princess Anne was born in 1950), with an extremely capable head on her shoulders. With the help of Prince Philip, her children, her advisers and, in recent years, an increasingly professional public relations office, she made the monarchy into one of the most popular and successful family businesses in the country.

The Queen's achievement has been remarkable. She has ridden out the inevitable let-down which followed the ridiculous talk of a "new Elizabethan age" in the fifties, taken the knocks of the swinging satirical sixties and resisted any suggestions that she abandon her stodgy love of corgis, horses and country pursuits for the sake of a trendier, more modern image. She is an astute woman who works hard at her job. Without being over-severe, she has brought to it a dignity and an application which is quite plainly appreciated by most of her subjects.

It is in contrast to her sister's unswerving devotion to her duty as Queen, wife and mother that Princess Margaret's willful behaviour has seemed so sadly deficient. It is against the background of an extremely carefully maintained code of royal conduct that Margaret has committed her transgressions. When Elizabeth told Margaret and Snowdon at the end of 1967 to "each go your own way—but please be quiet about it," she was offering more than mere sisterly advice.

The Queen's birthday celebration at Windsor on the evening of 20 April 1976 was marred by just one thing. This wasn't the absence of the newly-appointed Prime Minister James Callaghan who pleaded pressure of work. It was the presence at opposite ends of the ballroom of her sister, Princess Margaret and her brother-in-law, the Earl of Snowdon. One month and one day earlier amidst mounting gossip and speculation in the press throughout the world they had announced their legal separation. They had committed the one unforgiveable sin: they had permitted scandal to tarnish the blessed name and image of the Royal Family.

2

MARGARET BEFORE SNOWDON: CHILDHOOD AND THE TOWNSEND AFFAIR

Before her birth, Margaret's parents and family hoped and expected that she would be different. They wanted a boy.

George V had no grandsons in 1930, an omission that both the Royal Family and the public believed was due to be rectified. For while it was quite apparent that his eldest son, Edward, would succeed the 65-year-old George, it was not nearly so apparent that Edward would father the necessary male progeny to take over in a smooth and orderly fashion from himself. It was not at all certain, in fact, that Edward—by now in his mid-thirties, unmarried, and associating with no "suitable" woman—would have any legitimate children at all. This left Albert and Elizabeth's first daughter, Elizabeth, as the only viable third-generation heir to the Windsor throne, and Elizabeth's sex was the main reason why Albert and Mary were not rejoicing in that fact but rather praying that the embryonic Margaret would be a boy.

For the birth of her second child, Elizabeth surprisingly rejected the tall, terraced manse of Bruton Street—off Grosvenor Square—where she had given birth to Elizabeth, with its many conveniences and easy access to fine hospitals and doctors should complications set it. The Duchess even rejected her own official

London home at 145 Piccadilly, and insisted on moving that summer to Glamis Castle in Scotland. The Home Secretary, J. R. Clynes, who was obliged to attend the birth, could have been forgiven for assuming that as a member of Ramsey MacDonald's Labour Government he was being put to unnecessary trouble by the Yorks. The prospect of holing up in a hotel in nearby Perth throughout August, waiting for the call from Glamis, did not particularly appeal to him. As it happened, former millworker Clynes was finally housed at the tiny residence of Lady Airlie, and a makeshift telephone wire strung up between Glamis and Airlie Castle. Clynes later claimed that it was during the period of waiting that he came to love both the Scottish aristocracy and the scenery that they owned.

The locals, pleased at the prospect of a Scottish prince, prepared pipe-bands in the villages and bonfires on the hills. Tourists milled around the area, and the Great Bell of Forfar was primed. The expectant family tossed many names around between themselves: James, Charles, Henry. Any of those would be suitable for the newborn child.

At sunset on August 21, the telephone rang at Airlie Castle, and Clynes was told that he had an hour to reach Glamis, ten miles away as the crow flies, three times that much by rocky highland track. Clynes, however, was overcome by the romance of the journey, and seemed not to care that he arrived shortly after the child had been born. He was escorted to the billiard room and told gently on the way there that the little prince was not a little prince. He was a little princess.

The Bell of Forfar still chimed, fires were still lit, and for the sake of good manners the pipe-bands still played in Scotland and the men in London took off their hats and cheered as the news came through. *The Times* was less discreet. It announced: "There will be some natural disappointment that the baby is a girl and not a boy."

The parents were so disappointed that it was two weeks before they could decide on a name for their second daughter. When they did, it was Margaret Rose. They had briefly considered the name Ann, but George V would have none of it, and when the baby was transported to London to be christened at the end of October, Princess Margaret Rose it was.

If ever a child lived under the shadow of her elder sibling, that child was Princess Margaret. It was not easy for the young girl to understand, as toddler or teenager, the fact that her elder sister had all of the attentions befitting a future Queen of England lavished upon her, while Margaret was treated as merely the *sister* of the future Queen of England. When Edward abdicated, Margaret had only just learned to write her title: "York," and commented plaintively that now she was "Margaret of *nothing*." She frequently, as she grew older, accompanied Elizabeth on official outings, and would scour the papers later for the photographs—only to find, all too often, that sub-editors, pushed for space, had cut her out of them. Such treatment mortified Margaret and left her with a lingering sense that she must assert herself *more* in order to be noticed at all. Even a circular posted to Fleet Street, reading "Please do not cut Princess Margaret out of pictures unless unavoidable" did little to soothe her hurt spirits.

Margaret reacted to being forced to play second fiddle in a number of ways. Her obvious attempts to emulate Elizabeth turned out badly, and led her to mock many of the older girl's habits, such as her obsessive tidiness, and meek unwillingness to join in conversations. Margaret, by contrast, adopted a kind of promiscuous cheekiness, which came to be described by the press and by her sycophantic biographers as "roguishness." Later, this "roguishness" would become the cause of some embarrassment to her family, but for the moment it was explained away as pleasing and likeable high spirits.

Elizabeth and Margaret experienced the last of the fully cocooned royal childhoods. They were brought up in the confines of the family's London mansion at 145 Piccadilly, and rarely given the opportunity to meet children of their own age. They were not educated at any school, but trained in the niceties of royal life by a collection of nannies and governesses, the most prominent of these being Marion Crawford ("Crawfie"), who later left the service of the Royal Family and sold her none-too-flattering reminiscences to the American *Ladies Home Journal;*

and Margaret MacDonald ("Bobo") who still accompanies Queen Elizabeth everywhere and is regarded by many as her primary adviser—an exalted position that "Bobo" would certainly deny.

When the two sisters did leave the tall walls of 145 Piccadilly, it was hardly to mix with the crowds. They were once taken on a clumsily arranged journey on the London Underground, after their father had become King, perhaps as an ill-judged popularising gesture. Lady Helen Graham and Crawfie guided them, although neither of those two ladies had ever taken a tube ride before, and the journey from St. James's Park to Tottenham Court Road ended in confusion and an undignified dash away from pressmen into the nearest Young Women's Christian Association. A future proposal that "Lilibet," as Elizabeth came to be known, and Margaret should be taken on a bus ride was rejected by their father. The truth was that George VI did not really see the point in monarchy mixing with its people, except on official business. Later in his life, when his health was seriously threatened, it was suggested that he enter a hospital. George greeted this suggestion with a mixture of bafflement and umbrage: "I've never heard of a king going to a hospital before," he said. He was right, it had never happened. But before the next four decades were out, Kings, Queens and Princesses would find themselves in many unprecedented places.

1939 was an eventful year for the Windsors. In July, the 13-year-old Elizabeth was introduced to a gangling 19-year-old nephew of Lord Mountbatten's named Philip. The previous May, Philip had been vetted by Elizabeth's family at a tea party at Buckingham Palace. Elizabeth had not been there (though Margaret had), so nobody was quite prepared for the impression that this self-assured youth would make on her. Margaret, certainly, was amazed to see the dumbstruck expression on her sister's face as Philip was introduced to her in the captain's cabin of the royal yacht *Victoria and Albert* at Dartmouth. As one report would have it: "The colour drained from her face. Then it rediffused and went red. But she still stared at him, and for the rest of the day she followed him everywhere, glancing towards him with undiluted admiration."

Later on that day, Philip was larking around in a rowing

boat in the harbour following the *Victoria and Albert* out down-river, and was half-seriously shouted at by the adults on the royal yacht to beware of the choppy water. Margaret, turning to Eliza-beth, was startled to see tears of consternation running down her sister's face. Elizabeth had found her man.

It would be difficult to overstate the effect that Elizabeth's "love-at-first-sight" relationship with Philip had on the young Margaret. Once again, it seemed that the world had been de-signed to serve the future Queen, and to leave her younger sister grasping at the air. As a precocious 9-year-old, Margaret was well able to comprehend the fairytale romance of Elizabeth's being swept from her feet by a tall, blue-eyed, blond, and handsome sailor. It set a standard that she would have difficulty in living up to. In fact, of course, the Elizabeth-Philip affair was not *quite* as spontaneously glorious as that. They were introduced by Mountbatten, who later took care to see that Philip did not marry an attractive Canadian girl in 1943. But Margaret (or Elizabeth, for that matter) did not know of such things, and at the time it seemed as if elder sisters had *all* the luck.

As the nations of Europe embroiled themselves more deeply in the war with Germany, and it became obvious that despite Neville Chamberlain's thin finger in the dyke, Britain was going to be involved, the two girls and their mother were rushed north to Scotland. They spent all of that autumn and most of the winter of 1939 there, wondering why so cold and inactive a war had forced them from their home. "Who is this Hitler, and why is he spoiling everything?" Princess Margaret is reported to have petu-lantly exclaimed.

A week before Christmas, Queen Elizabeth's patience with the cold Scottish winter and frugal social life ran out, and she took her children to the traditional scene of royal seasonal fes-tivity: Sandringham.

After Christmas, the bombs began to fall, and the "little princesses" were moved first to the Royal Lodge at Windsor (where Margaret, described by a photographer at the time as "older than her years yet still showing a spontaneous self-assur-ance and a delightfully quick response" joined a local girl guide troop), and then as the bombing intensified to what was an-

The future Queen of England (left) with her younger sister, just after World War II

nounced as "a country house somewhere in England." This was actually the rather obvious Lancaster Tower of Windsor Castle, where the two sisters stayed, almost untouched by the war, until May 1945.

In November of that year Princess Margaret, unusually, attended the christening of the son of one of her father's Equerries of Honour. Wing Commander (as he was then) Peter Townsend had been born in India 31 years before, and had been an Equerry to George VI for only a little more than a year. He had gained during the war the kind of dashing, heady reputation for valour and flair that many fighter pilots acquired, and George VI had a policy of appointing wartime heroes as his Equerries. In 1941 Townsend had married, and this christening was of his second son. The Townsends lived "on the job," in Adelaide Cottage, a building tied to the Royal Estate at Windsor.

He had been recommended for the Distinguished Flying

Cross in the summer of 1943, about the same time that Margaret's wartime duties consisted of entertaining sixth-formers from the nearby Eton College in Lancaster Tower. (One pupil from that school, incidentally, who failed to get an invitation to take tea with the princesses because he was only in the lower school was a shy, small lad of good Welsh family, called Antony Armstrong-Jones.) But Townsend's qualifications for the post were shared by several other well-bred, heroic young men, and by the time George discontinued his practice of making them Equerries, he had more than were really necessary.

This meant that a couple of the younger, livelier ones were left with little else to do than entertain the royal children at Windsor. Townsend was helped in this task by a Lieutenant Peter Ashmore, a young bachelor from the navy who tried many times—in vain—to interest Margaret in fishing the River Dee. The truth was that although Ashmore could also play a decent game of tennis, Margaret was not particularly interested in him. The gentle eyes and modest, handsome smile of Peter Townsend carried far more charm for the King's younger daughter.

As a fifteen-year-old, though, she regarded Townsend, married and twice her age, as completely unobtainable. She certainly, at that age, harboured no designs on the man, even if she understood her feelings for him. But she was the King's daughter and used to having her way, and he was the King's employee and obliged to obey a Royal command, so Margaret saw as much of Peter Townsend as she wished—and that became a lot of the time.

As Elizabeth became more and more involved with Philip, spending most of the summer of 1946 with him at the Royal Lodge, Margaret was left increasingly alone and frustrated. The demands on Townsend's time accelerated, from simply riding through the park on balmy afternoons, to escorting her to the theatre in the evenings. Once, she even insisted that he sneak her into a local cinema. An affection between the two was growing, of this there can be no doubt, and the protestations—both at the time and later—by members of the Royal household that they could not "see anything going on" between the (lately promoted)

Group Captain and the Princess are hardly to be believed. More likely, they did not want to offend or cross in any way the notoriously sharp-tongued Margaret.

If the household must have recognised the developing relationship, however, the King and his immediate family certainly suspected nothing. Otherwise, Townsend would hardly have been left in such constant proximity to Margaret in England and Scotland, let alone been scheduled to accompany the Royal Family on their massive (February 1 to May 11) tour of southern Africa. As it was, Townsend and Peter Ashmore both travelled on the HMS Vanguard, and it was this gentle cruise through the seas of the southern hemisphere that cemented the nearly-17-year-old Margaret's love for Townsend, and that made Townsend finally realise that his hurried wartime marriage had been a sad mistake.

Accounts of that spring tour certainly sound idyllic, whether they mention the "alchemy about a voyage cut off from the prosaic world, sailing over the sea under wide skies, which has a way of titillating romantic thoughts," or of "delectable days beside the Indian Ocean," when Margaret galloped along the sands in the early morning with Peter Townsend.

Ironically, George VI was using this tour partly to test his other daughter's love for Philip, as a final check to see if it was no more than just a passing infatuation. He had never really been able to believe that Elizabeth could have been so single-minded in her devotion to one man from such an early age, but when the party returned to England, and she still declared her love for him, the King gave in. On 10 July 1947, the Palace announced the engagement of Princess Elizabeth to Philip. Although Margaret had known of its imminence, even people close to her could not help but comment on the effect that this liaison had on the volatile 16-year-old. "Something happened to Princess Margaret when Princess Elizabeth got engaged," remarked a friend. "She was never the same."

Margaret fell back heavily on the company of Peter Townsend but, finding that his unsure marriage was an obstacle to being with him in a discreet manner, launched herself into the wild London nightlife of her peers from the aristocracy; the young group of expensive partygoers that came eventually to be known, in newspaper shorthand, as "The Margaret Set." She had perhaps been advised—or maybe simply advised herself—that a future with Peter Townsend was impossible, and that the best way to forget any *idea* of such a thing was to hurl herself headlong into the maelstrom of clubs and all-night parties available to young ladies of her class and connections. She made friends, in these heady last few years of the 40's, that were to last for decades. Colin Tennant, the heir to Lord Glenconner, Sharman Douglas, the daughter of a rich Arizona businessman who was at the time U.S. Ambassador, Dominic Elliott, and more, were part of the "Margaret Set," and were still her close friends fifteen or twenty years later. That is a guide, not only to the fidelity of these people, but also to the limited circle in which Princess Margaret was able to move.

These times are rife with accounts of Princess Margaret seeing out her teenage years with gusto. The gossipy diarist, "Chips" Channon wrote of her in 1949, after seeing her at a party: "Princess Margaret was simply dressed. But already she is a public character, and I wonder what will happen to her? There is already a Marie Antoinette aroma about her . . ." Elder sister Elizabeth revealed that "She sleeps with the *Melody Maker* under her pillow." There are stories of can-cans in the U.S. Embassy, of imminent engagement to Dominic Elliott and any number of other dashing young things—Mark Bonham-Carter, Tom Egerton, Michael Tree. The names crop up regularly in the gossip columns of the time.

But the gossip columns of the time were either ignoring or had missed completely a story far bigger than any such flirtation in the 400 Club. In the background, always, was Peter Townsend, and compared to him these other flighty young men were temporary distractions. Her family, beginning to realise that all was not well in their younger daughter's heart, sent Margaret off on a variety of exotic, lengthy foreign holidays: to Italy, Switzerland, and Paris in 1949, to Malta with Elizabeth and Philip (who by now had produced the important male heir, Charles) in 1950. But Margaret returned unchanged and continued to pepper her lively social life with visits to Townsend.

She could not bear the fact of his being married to another

woman, even though the marriage had long since fallen into disrepair, Mrs. Townsend having met a neighbour at Windsor, a Mr. de Lazlo. Only, it seems, for the sake of their children did the Townsends try to hold their marriage together. For the sake of the children, they once tried to arrange a family holiday in France. They packed their suitcases, loaded the car, and were just about to leave when Margaret decided to step in. Unable to bear the idea of her Peter being away for a couple of weeks, she sent a message to him from Windsor Castle. It read: "Please attend Princess Margaret." Townsend did, and the holiday was cancelled.

The Townsends' marriage could not stand up to such strain, but there was no easy or obvious way out. The ghost of 1936 still haunted the Royal Family. It did not fade from view for many decades. In 1949, Elizabeth had made this clear when she referred to divorce as causing some of "the darkest evils in our society today." More than twenty years later, Prince William of Gloucester—the *ninth* in line of succession to the throne—told a journalist that one of the reasons he had never married was that he could not afford to make a mistake like his uncle. "Divorce is an unmentionable subject in our family."

Certainly, while his employer was fit enough to keep an eye on things, Townsend could not even *consider* divorce, or separation. George VI had virtually disowned his brother, packing him off to the Caribbean and vigorously opposing any suggestion that he should be invited back to Britain, even for just a brief visit. When George fell seriously ill in 1951, his immediate family managed somehow to blame the Duke of Windsor for *that*, suggesting that by abdicating his own regal responsibilities he had put too heavy a burden on George for a man to bear. They did not know that George was dying of lung cancer.

The King's obviously severe illness gave Townsend more freedom of movement. As it became clear towards the end of 1951 that George was unlikely to recover, Townsend's lawyers were told to begin drawing up the papers necessary to dissolve his marriage. On 6th February 1952, George VI died. Elizabeth and Philip were away in Kenya, and the young princess who was now second in line to the throne wept on the shoulder of Peter

Townsend. In May, they travelled together once more to South Africa, this time by aeroplane, and in November, Townsend's marriage was finally dissolved. His wife lost little time in marrying de Lazlo. Townsend's readjustment to bachelor life was to be rather less smooth.

As Margaret's friends from the late '40's "Set" got married, one by one, and as eligible young men from other European royal houses also slipped away from Margaret into the arms of matrimony, the press permitted itself some speculation about her future. She was only 22, but the absence of any obvious suitor, and the confusion of their previous speculations caused by the marriage of such eligibles as Johnny Dalkeith, made the gossip columnists curious. Margaret ignored their curiosity. It was by no means clear exactly how she was going to spend the rest of her life with Peter Townsend, but that is what she had determined to do.

As the coronation of Queen Elizabeth drew closer, Margaret and Townsend became more bold in their relationship, displaying mutual affection more openly than before. After the Christmas of 1952, one of the employees at Sandringham admits that the staff there spent some time wondering "whether a romance was developing between Princess Margaret and Peter. We watched what seemed to be a ripening friendship. Our view was that it would be regrettable if a man in Townsend's position allowed Princess Margaret's interest to grow into anything stronger than friendly feeling."

It was far too late. After one or two vain efforts to legitimise the "ripening friendship" by, for instance, having Townsend's mother to tea at Buckingham Palace, where the old lady noted approvingly that while Margaret called her son "Peter," Townsend never addressed the Princess as anything other than "Ma'am," Margaret announced to her sister and mother that she wanted—nay, *intended*—to marry Townsend. Why not? His divorced wife had been free to marry again, why could not a Princess of the Royal Family? And as the first half of 1953 ticked away, Margaret gradually eschewed any idea of keeping her affair with Townsend out of the public eye. At the coronation on June 2nd, she held his hand. This last gesture was noticed even by the press. Audrey

Whiting wrote in the *Daily Mirror* that Princess Margaret in the annexe of Westminster Abbey "was eagerly searching for someone. Who? Then I watched Peter Townsend hurry towards her—pushing aside noblemen and peers of the realm.

"I watched her brush a piece of cotton away from his RAF uniform. They were quite alone amid the most glittering gathering that I have ever witnessed. They were oblivious of everyone who surrounded them.

"Their hands touched briefly. It was such an intimate moment that I turned and walked away."

The new Queen was obliged, as one of her first chores in office, to take the unpleasant step of seeking the advice of Alan Lascelles and Prime Minister Winston Churchill about the possibility of her sister marrying a divorced man. They both insisted that such a move would be unconstitutional, would offend the church, and would do the Royal Family's public image a great deal of harm. The Queen Mother, annoyed by what she considered to be Townsend's lack of loyalty, echoed their verdict.

So the Royal Family prepared one of those carefully designed schemes to influence its members' lives that it had been perfecting for nearly a century. This time, however, the purpose of the scheme was to separate two lovers and not bring them together. Margaret, who had recently received a rise from the Civil List and was now drawing £15,000 a year from the state, was informed that marriage to Townsend would almost certainly mean sacrificing this allowance. Peter Townsend was given a choice between two jobs: one as air attache to the British Embassy in Brussels, and the other as air attache to the Embassy in Paris. He chose Brussels. The two lovers were told that a period of trial separation was necessary, but before that unhappy time they were to be allowed a holiday together in Rhodesia—the sugar coating of a bitter pill.

As it turned out, they had to swallow the pill unsweetened. *The New York Journal American* revealed, in early June, that Peter Townsend had been seeing too much of Princess Margaret. A week or so later, it emphasized its point by telling the world of Townsend's posting to Brussels. As the British press grudgingly picked up the pieces of a story that they'd been reluctant to investigate, Margaret and her mother flew to Rhodesia at the end of June—without Townsend.

On her return, Margaret submerged herself in a deep, lasting, and understandable self-pity. Townsend was not due to leave for Brussels until the end of October, but with the press sniffing more eagerly around, the chances of their meeting were severely curtailed. Margaret was 23 that August, she spent her birthday in an introverted mood at Birkhall, glancing occasionally at the picture of Townsend that she carried around with her, and initially refusing even to celebrate her birthday by going on a short picnic with Elizabeth and the children. It was becoming obvious to her that if her family had determined that she should not marry the divorcé, the press was helping hasten the end of her relationship with Townsend. It was no longer possible for her to forget about Royal protocol and assume that somehow, impossibly, things would all come right. Margaret was finally facing the reality of her situation, and it was not pleasant for her. Her relationship with Peter Townsend was beginning its drawn-out, stuttering end.

For the next two years, as a member of the Royal "Firm," Princess Margaret was of little use. She occasionally half-heartedly fulfilled an official duty, but she was quite apparently unsuited both in temporary mood and in permanent temperament to a position of such importance. And it *was* a position of importance, for under the Regency Act of 1937, had anything happened to Elizabeth then Margaret would have been Prince Charles' Regent until he was 21. The possibility of such an occurrence sent shivers down the spines both of her family and the government, and between them they rushed an amendment through Parliament, making Philip Regent. It was now virtually impossible for Margaret even to become Head of State, something that she did not particularly *regret*, but the fact that it was forced upon her must surely have hurt.

Throughout 1954, she mooned and dithered, still occasionally—*very* occasionally—seeing Townsend on his weekends in England, still carrying his picture everywhere, unable to agree finally to renounce him. She told her family that she would take a positive step when she was 25, and the word got around that by August 1955, the Townsend affair would have reached its final *dénouement.* To some of the press, this was not quite quick enough.

In February 1955, Margaret discovered the Caribbean Sea. On a tour of the West Indies, she was able to escape the tedium and depression that had become so large a part of her life back at Clarence House, London. Partying on the white sands with Noel Coward and Adlai Stevenson, swimming in the warm sea, she simply enjoyed herself more thoroughly and more consistently than she had done for many a long year. "We silly ones," she told the Chief Minister of Jamaica gaily, "will dance all night!"

She returned, at the beginning of March, to a harsher climate and to less sympathetic company. The British press was starting to demand that, in some way or other, she resolve the Townsend affair. As the year passed on and her twenty-fifth birthday approached, the clamour grew louder and more insistent, until two days before her birthday, when the *Daily Mirror* headlined: "COME ON MARGARET! Please Make Up Your Mind!" and filled its front page with a picture of her and the words: "For two years the world has buzzed with this question: Will

A drawn and weary Peter Townsend drives away from Clarence House shortly before Margaret officially renounces him

Princess Margaret marry 40-year-old Group Captain Peter Townsend? OR won't she?

"Five months ago, Group Captain Townsend told the *Daily Mirror*: '. . . the word cannot come from me. You will appreciate it must come from other people . . .'

"On Sunday the Princess will be 25 . . . She could end the hubbub. Will she please make up her mind?"

Crowds gathered around the small church at Balmoral when Margaret entered on her birthday, as if expecting some announcement from the pulpit, and in Brussels Peter Townsend was watched carefully by the press. They were all disappointed. No statement arrived. But the public's increased interest was not allayed by silence, and Margaret's family realised this.

On October 12, Townsend came to London. He met Margaret at Clarence House on the evening of the thirteenth. They were together all the following weekend at the Allanby Park estate of a distant relation, Mrs. John Wills, and spent most of the following week together at parties and dinner-dances. The weekend of the twenty-second saw them apart from each other for the first time in nine days, as Elizabeth and Philip tried once more to talk a decision out of Margaret at Windsor Castle. This time, they succeeded.

Margaret and Townsend spent October 29 and 30 together at the Uckfield home of friends. Margaret had already seen the Archbishop of Canterbury on the twenty-seventh, and told him that he could stop worrying, she had made up her mind. Now, to her family's and her advisers' displeasure, she insisted on issuing a public statement to the press. This sent Windsor Castle—at that time without any effective Public Relations Office—into a tizzy. Eventually, Margaret's statement was vetted, altered slightly, and on the 31 October 1955, it was issued.

"I would like it to be known that I have decided not to marry Group Captain Peter Townsend. I have been aware that, subject to my renouncing my rights of succession, it might have been possible for me to contract a civil marriage. But, mindful of the Church's teaching that Christian marriage is indissoluble, and conscious of my duty to the Commonwealth, I have resolved to put these considerations before any others.

"I have reached this decision entirely alone, and in doing so I have been strengthened by the unfailing support and devotion of Group Captain Townsend. I am deeply grateful for the concern of all those who have constantly prayed for my happiness.

"Margaret."

The Archbishop of Canterbury commented later: "When it became clear what God's will was, she did it, and that is not a bad thing for people in general to note." The press went through a brief period of contrition, congratulating Margaret on her wisdom, courage, and sense of duty, and wishing her luck on the "hard path" that she had chosen to tread.

Townsend returned to Brussels, and began making plans with a Belgian friend—a tobacco merchant from Antwerp named Jamagne—to travel around the world making a film travelogue. Margaret retreated back into Clarence House. Occasionally, she would venture forth into some social gathering or other. That December, for example, she went to see the trendy revue *Cranks,* the publicity photographs for which were taken by that young Etonian who had arrived at the school six years too late to meet Margaret over tea during the war: Antony Armstrong-Jones. In April 1956, she once more bumped into him as he took photographs at the wedding of her old friend Colin Tennant to Lady Anne Coke. But these were hasty affairs, and Margaret did not even engage in conversation with Armstrong-Jones. Her mind was still like her dressing table—littered with pictures of Peter Townsend.

In September 1956, Townsend lunched at Clarence House with Margaret and her mother and told them that everything was ready for his 60,000 mile trip. After he had left to traverse the globe, Margaret went on a trip to Africa. She returned to find the newspapers printing regular reports of his adventures, and went into another slight decline. She cancelled or simply failed to turn up at many official engagements throughout 1957, even missing her sister's tenth wedding anniversary celebrations. Occasionally, Townsend would telephone or write, and these brief interludes cheered Margaret up. But they *were* brief interludes, and her family worried about her physical and mental well-being. In March 1958, Townsend returned to London. Throughout that spring—except for a brief holiday in Trinidad—Margaret saw him frequently, at Clarence House and at the homes of friends. The press, naturally, reported these meetings with keen interest, and both Townsend and the Palace were obliged to issue statements, the former saying that things were still the same as in 1955, and the latter denying that an engagement was imminent.

Wearily, Margaret's family once more impressed upon her the importance of severing her links with Townsend, and that autumn, following a brief visit to Belgium where Townsend still lived, Margaret announced she would not see Townsend ever again.

Nearly a year later, in 1959, Peter Townsend married again. His wife was 21 years old, and the daughter of the Antwerp tobacco manufacturer who had travelled around the world in a Land Rover with Townsend. According to authorities like her Parisian hairdresser, Marie Luce Jamagne had an extraordinary facial resemblance to Princess Margaret. The couple settled down in the village of Rambouillet, near Paris, where Townsend wrote two books, one about his journey around the world, the other about the Battle of Britain, and worked in commerce.

He never did meet Princess Margaret again. His brother did, though, when she was touring Africa. As a witness recalls: ". . . she had to meet Townsend's brother. It was the rules of Empire. As a district officer in Africa, he was one of those who *had* to shake hands with a visiting princess. And there he was, the image of his brother.

"Only by chance, because it was something I would rather not have seen and it still haunts me, I happened to be standing near where the car with the princess in it was being driven away. By a similar coincidence, Francis Townsend happened to be by

*Group Captain Townsend and Marie-Luce Jamagne announce their be-
trothal to the world*

me at that time. She turned and saw him through the car's back
window. All the way up that African road a white face could be
seen staring and staring at this image of the man she loved until
the car disappeared . . ."

3

ENTER TONY ARMSTRONG-JONES

Antony Armstrong-Jones was born on 7 March 1930, just over five months before Princess Margaret. He is five feet, five and one-half inches tall, three and a half inches taller than Margaret. In both these respects he is strikingly different from Margaret's former great love, the mature and long-legged Peter Townsend. In attitude, as well, Armstrong-Jones is the antithesis of the conservative-minded and dutiful Group Captain who had bowed to protocol throughout his relationship with Princess Margaret.

Antony Armstrong-Jones was already a photographer when Margaret first met him, an unusual occupation for a product of Eton and Cambridge in the 1950's, and one from which his father had vainly attempted to dissuade him.

Tony Armstrong-Jones, despite his barrister father's air of respectability, came from a family of careerists. His father, Ronald, had been born plain "Ronald Jones" in 1899, and the aristocratic hyphenated "Armstrong-Jones" was acquired by grandfather Robert Jones who changed his name by deed-poll in 1913, "in order to avoid confusion with another Robert Jones." Ronald Armstrong-Jones, as he then became, subsequently brought off a considerable coup by marrying in 1925 Anne Messel, who became Tony's mother.

The Messels were an extremely wealthy banking family with close connections with the brightest and most aristocratic members of society. Ronald, a less than scintillating companion at the best of times, found himself hopelessly out of his depth in this marriage. "An apple pudding," said an onlooker at the time, "set in a souffle." The couple were divorced in February 1935. Tony's mother promptly married the Earl of Rosse, owner of 26,500 acres in Ireland and Yorkshire, in September of the same year and, in so doing, gave her six-year-old son an impressive demonstration of upward social mobility through marriage.

But it was more than just his mother's example that Tony Armstrong-Jones followed by making a prestigious marriage. The Jones side of the future Lord Snowdon's family shows, in fact, a remarkably consistent record of improving its station in life by making advantageous marriages. One hundred and fifty years ago, Lord Snowdon's ancestors, the Joneses, farmed an extremely small patch on an obscure Welsh hillside, and seemed likely to continue doing so. In the early part of the last century, however, two of the family, both called Thomas, father and son, contracted marriages to young ladies who happily chanced to come from families considerably better off than their own. Thomas junior married a Jane Elizabeth Jones (no relation) who, as an only child, passed on to her husband the considerable properties of the Eisteddfa estate on her father's death, four years after their marriage, in 1859. Their son Robert (who was later to change the family name "to avoid confusion") used the influence of his father's new-found position to get an education and eventually became a doctor.

Tony Armstrong-Jones' paternal grandfather, this Dr. Robert Jones, specialised in mental diseases. He became an authority on the subject and visited and experimented in lunatic asylums throughout Europe. He was also involved in the search to discover the identity of Jack the Ripper who, as has been suggested, was possibly connected with the Duke of Clarence, Princess Margaret's father's uncle.

Dr. Robert Jones inherited the family knack of recognising a good marriage prospect when he saw one. In his case it was Margaret Elizabeth Roberts, daughter of Sir Owen Roberts, a distinguished barrister and owner of considerable property including the estate of Plas Dinas in Wales. In 1899, when Ronald, Tony's father, was born, Sir Owen insisted that the boy be put down for Eton. When in 1913 the family name was changed from plain "Jones" to "Armstrong-Jones," Sir Owen signalled his approval by transferring the entire Plas Dinas estate to his daughter for a family home.

Dr. Robert Armstrong-Jones prospered. He became a Fellow of the Royal College of Surgeons and of the Royal College of Physicians. In 1915, he was knighted by George V for "treating shell-shocked soldiers." Father-in-law Sir Owen Roberts died in 1913, but young Ronald followed in the old man's footsteps, his way being considerably eased by family connections, and was called to the Bar in 1922. Ronald had at Eton met Linley Messel and been immensely impressed by the opulence and wealth of the Messel family house, Nymans, in Sussex. Linley happened to have a pretty elder sister, Anne, and Ronald married her in June 1925.

Anne Messel, Tony's mother and later Countess of Rosse, came from a family that was somewhat more distinguished than that of her first husband. The Messels had originally come from Germany in the middle of the last century to set up an English branch of their Darmstadt banking business that was much on the lines of the Rothschilds in nearby Frankfurt. Ludwig Messel, Anne's grandfather, was astute and extremely successful. In 1890, he bought the luxurious Sussex estate of Nymans as the most perfect type of English family home in which to live the life of an English country gentleman. His son, Leonard, went to Oxford and in 1902 brought the seal of English respectability to the family by marrying Maud Sambourne. Maud was the daughter of the very distinguished Linley Sambourne, a greatly respected artist and cartoonist who contributed to *Punch* for over forty years and was himself descended from the poet and playwright Richard Brinsley Sheridan.

Maud Sambourne brought an inestimable artistic cachet to the Messels. Her father's mansion in Kensington, 18 Stafford

Terrace (which is still owned by the Countess of Rosse) was a triumph of high-Victorian decoration. Together with Leonard Messel she restored Nymans to its extraordinarily sumptuous past glory as a sixteenth-century manor house, spending an immense amount of money importing old tapestries, porcelain, furnishings and valuable paintings, including a Velasquez.

Anne Messel was brought up at Nymans with her two brothers, Linley and Oliver, and at the highly prestigious 104 Lancaster Gate, overlooking Kensington Gardens. In 1922, Anne had been presented at Court to King George V and Queen Mary as one of that season's debutantes. Anne had been noted for her good looks and lively spirits. She particularly enjoyed the company of her younger brother, Oliver, a gay young thing at the Slade School of Art, and many of his unorthodox "artistic" friends.

The marriage of Anne Messel to Ronald Armstrong-Jones in 1925 was plainly a mis-match. She delighted in the most flippant and fashionable pursuits while he became increasingly stodgy as his career as a dutiful barrister drudged onwards across the South-Eastern Assizes, and was over-shadowed by his wife's bright friends. One of Leonard Messel's wedding presents had been 25 Eaton Terrace, which Anne had decorated in the very latest Syrie Maugham vogue of brilliant white with strong touches of colour. Here she would entertain her society friends like the Duchess of Westminster, Lady Diana Cooper, Lady Edwina Mountbatten, the Countess of Seafield (the richest woman in England), Sir Michael Duff, Colonel Wingfield Digby, not to mention Cecil Beaton, Noel Coward and other of brother Oliver's odd friends.

Ronald Armstrong-Jones was sinking fast under all this. The birth of a daughter, Susan, in 1927 did little to cool his wife's ardour for party-going. On 7 March 1930, she gave birth to a boy, Antony. The future Lord Snowdon was christened in a very lavish ceremony at the Temple Church. He had no less than seven godparents: Sir Michael Duff, Colonel Wingfield Digby, Nigel Gibbes, Elaine Wauchope, Lady Forres, Lady North and the Countess of Seafield. Among the christening presents given to the baby were two gold pins.

What young Antony Armstrong-Jones was not to receive,

however, was much attention from his parents. His father worked long hours and when not working would go off on his own alone, fishing or shooting. His mother became even more caught up in the whirl of London society and, additionally now, in the theatrical career of brother Oliver as stage designer for the prodigious producer C. B. Cochran.

Young Tony grew up under the care of his nanny, Laura Gunner, who provided the only stability in his early childhood. Before he was three Tony's parents separated, and Ronald took a house at 6 Trevor Square, near Harrods, where he installed Nanny Gunner and Tony with sister Susan.

Like Ernest Simpson in 1936, Ronald Armstrong-Jones allowed his wife to petition him for divorce on the grounds of his adultery with an unnamed "other woman" in a seaside hotel. One afternoon in March 1934, while waiting for the case to come up and with the children away with their mother at Nymans, Ronald's white bulldog ran off the lead and chased a black cocker spaniel down the steps of 24 Trevor Square. When Ronald rang the bell to ask for his dog back, he was delighted to find the door opened by a petite blonde named Carol Coombe. She was twenty-two, he was thirty-five. She was a small-time actress and Ronald Armstrong-Jones suddenly became interested in the theatre. Her career—not altogether surprisingly—failed to blossom, but their friendship did.

Tony's parents were divorced on 22 February 1935. For his fifth birthday on March 7, which he spent at Plas Dinas, he received a pony called Ladybird. He didn't see either of his parents. His mother spent the day at a society wedding in London, and his father was with Miss Coombe. A governess, Madelaine Martin, known as "Marty," was engaged, and she took on the job of helping Nanny Gunner look after the two children until they were old enough to be sent away to school.

At Nymans during the summer of 1935, Tony became increasingly aware of the visits of the handsome twenty-nine-year-old Michael Parsons, Earl of Rosse. His mother was then thirty-three. That September she married Parsons, becoming Countess of Rosse. The wedding was—predictably—awash with socialites. Less lavish was the ceremony at Westminster Registry Office in

June the following year when Tony's father married Carol Coombe. From then on the parents shared the children, more or less equally.

Tony's mother's new home was Birr Castle in Ireland. An immense piece of Gothic stone-masonry in verdant grounds, it provided Tony with a stunning visual display of what could be achieved by a judicious marriage. Back in England, his father and stepmother found it difficult to keep up with the Rosses. They started taking Tony to the theatre in London, *Peter Pan* especially taking his fancy. With the encouragement of his stepmother, Tony began to indulge in a taste for dressing up and for experimenting with makeup which were long to keep their attractions for him.

Deprived of regular parental attention, Tony became withdrawn and demanding. The jolts of moving from one parent's home to the other and back again every few months developed in him a capacity to adapt to different situations and to adopt different postures in order to get what he wanted. Early on, he became secretive, wily, and inclined to be moody when crossed. The birth to his mother of two boys, one in 1937 and the other in 1938, required his presence at Birr at two baptismal services at which he was very far from the centre of attention. He now had more pressing rivals for his mother's affection. When he was eight-and-a-half he was packed off to his first boarding school. This was Sandroyd, an expensive prep school in Surrey which specialised in getting boys into Eton or Harrow. It had all the barbaric practices which young English public schoolboys are encouraged to indulge in. The ice-cold baths and sadistic dormitory rituals of initiation came as a highly unpleasant contrast to the cosseted regimes of Nanny Gunner and Governess Marty.

Never a bookish child, Tony also found for the first time—and by no means for the last—that his diminutive stature was a handicap to him. A school report describes him as "not particularly brilliant . . . too small to be much good on the playing fields." He did attempt to box, however, in a specially created flea-weight division. The school magazine describes his efforts as showing "a good deal of pluck in taking punishment and coming up again smiling."

The 8-year-old Tony (right) with his mother—by then Countess of Rosse—on a Christmas visit to Birr Castle, Ireland

Tony was not popular with his school friends. Nor did his scholastic achievements win approval from the staff at the school or from his parents. While at Sandroyd, Tony Armstrong-Jones was always near the bottom of his class in Latin, English, French and mathematics.

For the duration of the war, Sandroyd was evacuated to an old house on the Wiltshire-Dorset border. The move did little to improve Tony's lacklustre school record. The only advantage he seems to have taken of the wartime exigencies was when he persuaded his stepmother, at a time when so many household servants had gone into the services, to allow him to dress up as a parlour maid and serve dinner to his father and grandfather at Plas Dinas. His father was not amused.

The difficulties of wartime travel meant that Tony saw less and less of his mother. His father was then posted with the King's Royal Rifles and went around the country acting as Judge Advocate at courts martial. This meant that Tony did not see his father even during his vacations. Tony increasingly became a lonely, isolated boy, forming only with great difficulty even the most tenuous of friendships with other children.

Tony scraped into Eton in the Michaelmas term of 1943. So small was he for his age that he had to suffer the indignity of wearing a short jacket instead of an Eton tailcoat throughout his schooldays. He continued his undistinguished record he had begun at Sandroyd. One Eton master laconically wrote on an end of term report: "Maybe he is interested in some subject but it is not a subject we teach here." There seemed little hope that Tony would follow his father into law. Perhaps he might be interested in medicine? To this end Tony was given grandfather Sir Robert Armstrong-Jones' old microscope but this failed to fire his imagination. Tony polished it, put it up on his bookshelf and left it there.

Early in 1944, however, Tony was taken out for the afternoon by his grandmother Maud Messel. After lunch she took him to the house of her artist father Linley Sambourne at 18 Stafford Terrace which had recently passed to her from her brother. Tony was entranced by its Victorian elegance. But he was even more stunned when shown the studio at the top of the house containing a collection of 13,000 photographs accumulated by Linley Sambourne for the detailed backgrounds of his *Punch* drawings. That did it. Back at Eton, Tony swapped his grandfather's precious old microscope for another boy's box camera and embarked upon the life-long love of photography which was to lead to his marriage to the sister of the Queen of England.

Tony's academic record at Eton showed no signs of improving. He did, nevertheless, persevere with his boxing and eventually managed to obtain sufficient proficiency to win a few fights. In 1946, however, when he was sixteen, Tony Armstrong-Jones was suddenly struck down with polio during the worst epidemic ever known in England. His mother flew over from Ireland, and his uncle Oliver Messel came up from London. His mother wrote, "I could foresee nothing but a crippled life in front of him, even should he recover."

Tony spent six months in the Liverpool Royal Infirmary. His back and left leg were severely affected, but Tony's innate stubbornness and determination ensured that he made a steady and unexpectedly speedy recovery. He emerged with a limp, which he manages to conceal more or less successfully, from one leg being slightly shorter than the other. While largely bed-ridden for those six months Tony underwent his true education. He learned to become even more self-reliant. Frequently visited by uncle Oliver Messel, then designing for Covent Garden and Glyndebourne, Tony was taught about stagecraft and model-making. Oliver encouraged Tony in his ever-growing interest in photography. Tony used his time in hospital to gain a thorough knowledge of the workings of every conceivable type of camera and when allowed up would take whatever photographs he could.

Back at Eton, having discarded wheelchair, crutches and sticks, Tony founded the Eton Camera Club and submitted for an exhibition a photograph of the re-building of Upper School which had been bombed in 1940. The entry was not well received. "The picture might well have been made more exciting if there had been signs of human activity," said one review of it. Tony, characteristically, stuck the critical report in a scrapbook. Throughout his career Tony Armstrong-Jones has maintained this practice of saving adverse notices of his work. He does not take criticism easily and will not easily forgive or forget those who have been uncomplimentary about him.

Tony was able to assert himself sufficiently by the summer term of 1947 to obtain the coveted position of cox for his House's boat on the important Fourth of June races. King George VI and his family, including Princess Margaret, paid a visit to Eton a fortnight after this personal triumph, and so gave Tony Armstrong-Jones a second opportunity (the other had been during a royal visit in 1943 when he was only in his first year), to gaze upon his future wife.

Tony Armstrong-Jones left Eton at the end of the summer term of 1948. His career there had not been spectacularly successful. That autumn he was rejected for national service. He later recalled with studied casualness: "I was graded something like ZZZ, which meant that if people over 90 were called up then I would be too, and oddly enough I minded that grading very much. I never escaped the feeling that I had missed out on National Service."

In the meantime, however, his stepfather at Birr Castle and his father at his new home at Combe Place provided him with dark rooms and cameras and photographic equipment with which to keep him occupied. Tony was solitary and secretive and playing about with cameras seemed to be the only thing that kept him happy.

A place was eventually found for him at Cambridge. In October 1948, Tony went up to Jesus College. Just what he proposed to study proved something of a problem, given that he displayed no interest whatever in learning anything. First, Natural Sciences was decided upon, but ten days later he switched to Architecture. But this change didn't do him much good, and he was sent down at the end of his second year after having repeatedly failed his exams.

At Cambridge, as at Eton, Tony Armstrong-Jones failed to shine. Apart from failing exams and one photographic contribution to the university magazine "Varsity," his one achievement was to cox the winning Cambridge boat in the Oxford and Cambridge boat race of 1950. A few heads were turned by Tony's sweater emblazoned with his full initials, A.C.R.O.L.A.J., but in the excitement of Cambridge's comfortable victory this display of "swank" was forgiven him.

Failing his exams and being sent down was a very considerable blow. Then his sister was married on 20 May 1950 to John Vesey, the Viscount de Vesci and owner of considerable property and position in Ireland. All around Tony were the trappings of success and wealth, while he seemed to be going nowhere. He was still supposed to become an architect, but he was only too aware of his lack of ability in that field. What he enjoyed doing was taking photographs, but could that be a career? In a long letter to his mother at Birr Castle in which he cited the example of Cecil Beaton, Tony expressed his desire to take photographs for a living. Lady Rosse replied with a curt telegram: "Do not agree suggestion changing career. Telephone this evening. Fondest love, Mummy."

In August, Tony went over to Birr Castle with Uncle Oliver and Lord Rosse, who convinced Tony's mother to look more sympathetically upon the idea, but all agreed that Tony's father would be less easily persuaded. Back in London Tony went through a miserable time. Nothing went right. He decided, for example, that he was in love with Lady Barbara North and vainly attempted to ingratiate himself with her. But she married another man, Clive Bossom, the following year, and Tony had to content himself with taking the wedding photographs.

After about three months Tony became incredibly depressed. According to his stepmother it became impossible to wake him in the mornings, and he would mess up any job interviews his father set up for him, among them one with a wine merchant and another with the head of a tobacco firm. A meeting was arranged with the directors of his mother's family stockbroking business, the Messels, but according to Tony: "I had lunch with the directors, and as far as I can remember I left before the pudding; I just knew the City wasn't for me."

Ronald Armstrong-Jones finally suggested that his son be apprenticed to an architect's office. To this Tony replied: "You'll be wasting your money. I don't want to work at something I'm not really interested in. I must be frank. I've been thinking all this time, and now I'm certain. I know that will be a shock to you, but all I want to be is a professional photographer."

Ronald recognised his son's stubborn streak. "We must see what we can do then," he said. He was as good as his word.

From November 1950, Ronald Armstrong-Jones provided Tony with a £200 a year allowance, the free use of his flat in the Albany and then, later, with £1,000 with which to set up a studio of his own. To begin with, Tony operated from a dark room in the Albany, printing private portrait photographs to use as Christmas cards. His first client was an actress friend of his stepmother's called Helena Pickard, and she placed an order for a hundred cards. Some time passed, then Tony received a second, but considerably smaller, order from another actress, Joan Morton, for some portrait photographs of her cats. Tony wasn't really getting very far.

Tony needed to find an established leading photographer who would be prepared to take him on as a pupil. Cecil Beaton, uncle Oliver Messel's close friend, was ruled out since he didn't operate from a proper studio. But luckily enough, another of Tony's stepmother's friends was very friendly with Baron, the leading royal photographer of the day. Baron was invited round to the Albany for drinks to meet the aspiring young photographer. Baron, who was not immune to the physical charms of members of his own sex, agreed to take on Tony as a student for a fee of five hundred guineas.

The time that Tony spent at Baron's smart studio gave him an extremely thorough introduction into the technicalities of portrait photography as well as providing him with unrivalled opportunities for making social contacts. Tony didn't waste his time and worked hard on both of these fronts. After six months Baron was sufficiently impressed by Tony's proficiency and continued enthusiasm that he offered him an extended period of training, not as a fee-paying assistant but at a nominal salary.

While with Baron, Tony also undertook a number of freelance engagements as a society photographer. Occasionally, he would cause acute embarrassment to his family, for instance, when he appeared one evening at Claridge's with cameras slung

Tony in his bachelor days

around his neck to take photographs of Princess Marie Louise who happened to be seated at the top table with his father and step-mother. Tony was quite shameless in utilising these family connections to get a set of pictures of the old lady who normally refused to be photographed.

Certain of Tony's contemporaries looked less than favourably upon his activities. After one party at the Savoy a group of fellow Old Etonians set upon him and debagged him. He was later found unconscious in some bushes. When he had recovered he said:

"It may have been funny to some. To me it was unforgivable. It seems that it is rather infra dig to be in society and a photographer at the same time. It seems I should be a stockbroker or someone stinko with money." Tony never forgot such snubs. Their effect was to increase his determination to succeed.

For his twenty-first birthday in 1951, Tony Armstrong-Jones was provided by his father with a small flat of his own in the Albany. Tony here carried out the first of his idiosyncratic excursions into bizarre forms of interior decoration. He made maximum use of his limited space and money by filling the flat with not-yet fashionable bits of Victoriana and junk. He began to dress a little wildly, wearing scarlet-lined evening capes and the like. He became more confident about his professional abilities. It became clear to him that the moment had come to try to make it on his own.

With a friend, David Sim, Tony set up a studio at 59 Shaftesbury Avenue in the summer of 1951. He remained there for two years and developed a reputation as an inventive and original young photographer.

To begin with, however, there was extraordinarily little demand for inventive or original photography. Tony easily got to see the editor of the arch-traditional *Tatler*, who was not one to pass up a good thing when he saw one. But it was on account of Tony's social connections, not innovative ideas, that Sean Fielding welcomed his work.

From September 1951, photographs by "A. Armstrong-Jones" began to adorn the pages of the magazine. The subjects of these photographs, unsurprisingly, turned out to be almost exclusively Tony's family, who somewhat reluctantly agreed to be roped in to helping the boy get on. The captions beside the photographs were unashamedly snobbish and sycophantic: "Mrs. Messel photographed in her charming drawing room . . . looking at some pictures which her son, Oliver Messel, sent to her on her birthday recently"; "The Countess of Rosse in the Gothic Saloon at Birr Castle looking at a photograph album with her son, Lord Oxmantown"; "The Countess of Rosse waving farewell to departing guests after a houseparty of young people at Birr."

Uncle Oliver Messel gave Tony the entré to a theatrical party at Claridge's thrown by Laurence Olivier and Viven Leigh, which enabled him to grace the pages of the *Tatler* with pictures of all the theatrical lights of the day. Early in 1952, Tony's mother got him the highly prestigious job of photographing Princess Georg of Denmark for the *Tatler*, a full-page feature, the sort of thing which usually was done by Baron.

But Tony was already straining at the bit. He vainly attempted to get pictures into other, less rarified, magazines like *Picture Post* or even into *Country Life*. He invariably got turned down and seemed destined to continue doing only society photographs of his family or of his family's social circle for the *Tatler*.

He endeavoured to expand his own social circle, mixing business with pleasure. He took photographs of Old-Etonians like Anthony Tennant and of gay blades like Jeremy Fry and Dominic Elwes. Taking his cameras with him, Tony would frequently be seen at nightspots like Ciro's Club or the Carousel where the most sparkling and brightest young things were to be seen. Tony was very far from being the center of attention at such gatherings. As one observer commented: "He seemed to know people rather better than they knew him." Occasionally, he did actually relax and enjoy himself, although he chose—at times—some odd ways in which to do so, for example, when he turned up in full drag at a Belgravia mews party.

At the end of 1952, he came across a disused ironmonger's shop at 20 Pimlico Road which he converted into a highly unorthodox and amusing studio where he entertained his friends and sitters. Shortly before Christmas, Tony held a studio-warming party for twenty-two people, including Clarissa Chaplin and Sally Churchill, David and Anthony Tennant, Gina North, Dominic Elwes, Davina Portman, Mary Williamson and Robert Erskine. Instead of place cards the guests were seated before photographs of themselves taken by Tony. A young man in Spanish costume strummed a guitar, the table was decorated with out-of-season lilacs, and later on, a cabaret of Spanish dancers entertained the company with castanets and flamenco.

In 1953, Coronation Year, Tony went to Eton at the beginning of term and took candid camera shots of tearful farewells and nervous youngsters (including his own half-brother Martin Parsons) unpacking their luggage. Once again *Picture Post* turned him down, but *Tatler* published the pictures. Tony received an extremely sharp letter of rebuke from the headmaster of Eton for having taken the photographs without permission. Tony stuck the letter into his scrapbook and went on looking for new projects.

While trying hard to break out of the *Tatler* mould, Tony did not fail to take advantage of the prestige provided by his by-line appearing so regularly in its pages. Debutantes flocked along to his studio and Tony's prices duly went up and up. In fact, the more expensive he became, the more in demand he was. But this kind of success was not enough. He recalled, "In those days, they were lit by two spots from behind, and a light under the nose to make the cheeks a bit thinner, and then an inky-dinky spotlight in front, just to give a little sparkle in the eyes. This had nothing to do with photography."

Then in 1954, Oliver Messel provided Tony with the sort of break he was looking for. Oliver introduced him to the producer, Peter Glenville, who invited him to take publicity photos for a new Terence Rattigan play, *Separate Tables*, starring Margaret Leighton. Instead of the usual static photo-calls, Tony insisted on taking action shots of the play during rehearsal performances and then had these blown up to almost life-size and placed outside the theatre. The object, he said, was to make people stop, look and go into the theatre to buy seats for the show. The photographs were so successful that Tony was immediately commissioned to do the publicity shots for a string of other shows in the West End. There wasn't a great deal of money in it as yet, but Tony had the satisfaction of working with theatrical types with whom he felt much more affinity than with the more boring aristocratic patrons he would normally get at his studio.

There is some conflict of evidence as to Tony's private life at this time. His assistant at his Pimlico studio, Keith Croft, who was fifteen and fresh out of school, paints a picture that is almost too highly coloured of a vigorously heterosexual man-about-town: "In the deb season it was almost one continuous party. We'd have half a dozen different girls in for sittings every week and nearly always Tony would persuade them to stay on for a party after the day's work. They seldom objected. There were always guests staying the night at the studio. One of my first jobs each morning was to make coffee for them."

Tony's stepmother began to be a little worried: "He tended to choose his friends from people not known for their prowess on the sports field, but because of their artistic qualities or attitudes. In this world—sometimes a half-world—of the arts, from the darker frontiers of the stage and photography, many strange characters abounded, odd in dress and outlook. It was unfortunate that because of his glancing association with them he has sometimes—quite wrongly—been judged to be one of them." Tony Armstrong-Jones certainly enjoyed the company of many homosexuals and made no secret of the fact that he revelled in dressing up and in other "unmanly" pursuits. As late as the 1970's he would be greeted at parties by people like Lord Lambton with cries of "Christ, I can smell the bugger's scent from here!" And in July 1971, after a fracas with Peter Cazalet, the Queen Mother's horse trainer, Cazalet contemptuously turned his bottom towards the then Lord Snowdon saying, "I'm going to show you the only part of me you'd be interested in!"

In 1955, Tony acquired the basement underneath his studio in Pimlico Road. He took enormous pleasure in a spiral staircase that connected it with the studio and was predictably inventive in furnishing an elegant, slightly unorthodox new home for himself. He became an accomplished host, able to put guests from many different backgrounds at their ease. He cultivated a charm which when necessary positively oozed.

Sensing a trend, he began experimenting with fashion photography. He would place haute couture clothes against scrap heaps, snap models slipping on banana skins or haughty women peering hungrily into shop windows. He often went to great expense taking such photographs, and he was not always successful in selling them. But he now had the confidence to know when and how to push and was prepared to wait for the correct moment at which to get his foot well and truly in the fashion door.

Fellow-dandy Mark Boxer, who knew Tony from Cambridge, speaks of his "quickness, his sensitivity, his cheek, his sense of timing, his inquisitive interest in people," which were fast making him one of the most original photographers working in England.

He also became even more audacious about getting a picture he wanted. In the autumn of 1955, for example, he managed to get a set of pictures of the re-opening of the Vienna Opera House by sending in a bouquet of yellow roses to the leading soprano, Sena Jurinac, then while on the point of being thrown out, yelling to her from the wings, "I'm the man who sent the roses." He charmed the singer and got his pictures.

Tony's circle was increasingly chic: actors and actresses, artists, dancers, interior decorators, all swarmed in and out of his life. He took to having the more celebrated of them autograph a mirror in his Pimlico Road house with a diamond. In 1954, he met the exotic, if tiny, Eastern beauty and actress Jacqui Chan with whom he was frequently romantically linked over the following four years, although they both consistently stuck to the "no marriage—just good friends" line.

It was with a batch of photos of Jacqui Chan that Tony approached *Vogue* in early 1956, having decided that the time was right to crack the fashion scene. The then editor, Penelope Gilliat, didn't think much of Miss Chan but took up two of his other pictures for publication in the very next issue.

This was the beginning of an immensely successful business relationship between Tony Armstrong-Jones and *Vogue* which was to last up until his marriage. Tony brought enthusiasm and invention into a previously rather stuffy institution. By March 1957, he was rivalling Norman Parkinson in the field of colour fashion photography.

This sort of success would doubtless have satisfied a less ambitious man than Tony Armstrong-Jones. But he was simply not content to be restricted to any one sphere of activity. He continued to pursue all the other branches of his photographic career. In fact, he embarked upon a crucially new one. In 1956, Baron died. This created a gap in the rank of royal photographers. Tony Armstrong-Jones carefully manoeuvred to fill this gap.

In June 1956, Tony wrote to the Queen's cousin, the Duke of Kent, whose twenty-first birthday was imminent, suggesting that he might take the official birthday portraits. Tony had met the Duke of Kent through a mutual friend, Jane Sheffield, and they had both been present at Jane's wedding to Jocelyn Stevens, one of Tony's friends from Cambridge. Additionally, the Duke frequently went dancing with Emma Tennant, whose cousin Tony also knew well.

Tony got the commission, and his formal portrait of the Duke in the full-dress uniform of the Royal Scots Greys was extremely successful. The Queen saw the photographs, liked them and arranged to be introduced to Tony Armstrong-Jones later that summer at a cocktail party at the Uckfield house of the Nevill

The young photographer outside his Pimlico studio. Aston Martins came later

family. (It was the same house in which Princess Margaret and Peter Townsend had spent their last weekend together in October of the previous year.) Tony happened to have taken some pictures of the Nevill children, Guy and Angela, and the Queen was favourably impressed by them. A couple of months later, Tony received a 'phone call from Commander Colville, the Queen's press secretary, who asked whether he would like to photograph Prince Charles and Princess Anne. Tony took his cameras and lights along to Buckingham Palace and overnight became a national name.

Hitherto, photographs of the Royal Family had been stiff, formal affairs emphasizing the pomp and dignity of the monarchy. Tony Armstrong-Jones changed all this, and replaced it with a carefree, relaxed and more natural approach. And he was not afraid to use occasional bold touches, such as photographing Charles and Anne in silhouette on either side of a large globe (which he had brought with him in the back of his car) against a bleached-out background.

The photographs created an enormous amount of public interest. They were unconventional, they were dazzling. Newspapers canvassed professional opinions as to the merits of Tony's work. Their views were predictable: "Terribly posed. No life or character in it." "Absolutely rotten. I'd tear it to pieces." "Bad composition." "I don't think it will be popular in America." and the inevitable "It's just not the way to take pictures of Royalty."

Tony was controversial. He was labelled "photographer Royal" and "golden new boy of the watch-the-birdie trade." His background was explored in the newspapers, and columnists were delighted to find in him a chirpy, bright and energetic young man who was only too eager to cooperate in providing them with material for their features. His Pimlico studio, his theatrical friends, his modest demeanour . . . It was all trotted out and lapped up. At the age of twenty-six Tony had most certainly arrived.

Commissions flooded in. More surprisingly, the commissions themselves became news. The following year, for example, the *Daily Mail* carried a *full page* feature on Tony Armstrong-Jones in France shooting stills for the re-make of "A Tale of Two Cities." He was photographed flying out to Geneva to photograph the wedding of the Sadruddin Khan. He delighted newspaper readers with his informal photographs of the Queen and Princess Anne on the latter's seventh birthday in August 1957. He did some judicious retouching of Princess Alexandra's twenty-first birthday pictures in December. Everything he did was news.

In June 1957, Tony staged his first one-man show at Kodak House in Kingsway. He went all out for spectacular effects. Using huge blow-ups, the like of which had not been seen in a photographic exhibition before, he filled, or over-filled, the entire hall with examples of his best work from the past five years. He put pictures together in a bizarre juxtaposition. An ancient peasant woman from Madeira would be next to a couple in morning dress at Ascot. A mural of ballerina Anya Linden nineteen feet high would lead on to close-ups of bleak Yorkshire slum life. Three-times life-size portraits of Eartha Kitt, Harold Macmillan and Tommy Steels loomed down on visitors. More pictures were built into boxes, tables and stools.

Inevitably, gossip-writers wanted to dish the dirt, but try as they might all they could find out about Tony's private life was that he was an "absolute charmer," had "perfect manners" and "possessed the gift of making any woman—pretty or plain— feel that she is the loveliest and most desirable girl at a party." Nebulous stories went the rounds about a friendship with Sarah Rothschild which was supposed to have "blossomed in Venice." There was an even more fatuous one concerning an oil heiress called Olga Deterding. This one purportedly had ended when "Olga threw up everything to work for Albert Schweitzer in his famous African colony for lepers."

The columnists really had their work cut out for them. Small wonder, then, that they made such a fuss over the one real romance in Tony Armstrong-Jones' life that he didn't attempt to conceal, the one with Jacqui Chan. The press eagerly reported that in June 1958 he drove "eighteen miles" from his Pimlico home to greet his half-Chinese showgirl friend. "He swept her up in his arms, hugged her and smothered her cheeks with kisses." In January of the following year it was her turn to greet him at the airport. "She is still the girl in his life," said the newspapers.

Little did the press know that the charming "royal photographer" had already embarked upon a royal friendship with Princess Margaret and was using his relationship with Jacqui Chan, which had peaked in 1956, as a smoke-screen.

Tony Armstrong-Jones had seen Princess Margaret twice while at Eton, but she only became aware of his existence in April 1956, when he took the photographs at the wedding of her friends, Colin Tennant and Anne Coke at Holkham Hall. She had only barely noticed him even then. Since that wedding, however, Tony had become something more than just a society photographer. One of Margaret's extra ladies-in-waiting, the lively Lady Elizabeth Cavendish, daughter of the Duke of Devonshire, had known Tony through society and theatrical circles for some time. She found him charming, witty and attractive. She was to encourage him in many ways. Lady Elizabeth was four years older than the Princess and had accompanied Margaret on her Caribbean tour of 1955, seeing her through the Townsend crisis. Lady Elizabeth was also one of the backers of the successful revue *Cranks*, for which Tony Armstrong-Jones took the front of house photographs, and to which she took Princess Margaret in February 1956.

Lady Elizabeth Cavendish also accompanied Margaret down to Holkham Hall for the Tennant wedding that April. She didn't get the opportunity to formally introduce Tony to the Princess there. She was, in fact, more immediately successful in bringing Tony together with other members of the Royal Family. It was Elizabeth Cavendish who prompted Tony to take the photographs of the two Nevill children that the Queen saw at Uckfield that summer and which led to him receiving his first commission from Buckingham Palace.

Lady Elizabeth Cavendish finally formally introduced Tony Armstrong-Jones to Princess Margaret at a dinner-party which she gave at her mother's Chelsea house, 5 Cheyne Walk, in February 1957. By then Princess Margaret could hardly have been unaware of just who Tony was. Not altogether surprisingly, Margaret found him charming, witty and attractive. From then on, Tony found himself regularly included as one of the Princess' party at theatre or dinner gatherings, but discreetly, so as not to bring their growing acquaintance to the attention of the public. In July 1957, Margaret, accompanied again by Elizabeth Cavendish, paid her first visit to Tony's Pimlico Road studio. There she saw the dismantled pictures from his Kodak House exhibition and was intrigued by the combination of bric-a-brac and chic that he had assembled.

But a greater surprise awaited Margaret and, again, this was something that Lady Elizabeth Cavendish knew about before the Princess did. It was the existence of a secret hideaway that Tony had found in 1956. This was a small riverside house at 59 Rother-hithe Street, an unfashionable cul-de-sac about a mile down-stream from Tower Bridge on the south bank. Tony had persuaded a journalist named Bill Glenton who owned the house to let him convert part of it for his own private use.

The work involved in creating an inhabitable living-area of what was virtually a ruin was considerable. But Tony excelled himself. With rush matting on the floor, fresh paint and scoured beams, the room overlooking the river took on a fresh life. Tony installed an eclectic collection of furniture, from old rocking chairs to ancient divans, and generally cluttered up the place with the sort of old rubbish that was beginning to be fashionable again. Tony had created a delightful, slightly mysterious and undeniably romantic little pied-a-terre.

Above all the place was totally secluded and totally cut off from the world outside. In other words, it offered the kind of privacy that Princess Margaret had never in the whole of her life been able to enjoy. In March 1958, muffled up and wearing a headscarf, she crossed the river incognito to join Tony Armstrong-Jones for drinks at 59 Rotherhithe Street.

4

THE COURTSHIP OF
MARGARET AND TONY,
THEIR MARRIAGE PRE-1972

The decline of mental and physical health which Margaret suffered after her final renunciation of Peter Townsend worried both
her family and her friends. The migraines which for years had
only occasionally bothered her now intensified, leaving her racked
with misery for days. Her chain-smoking, which doctors had
been warning her about for years, showed no sign of easing
up. For months Margaret was a lonely, unhappy figure hidden
inside the walls of Clarence House, rarely fulfilling either social
or official functions. "God knows," said one friend to another at
the time, "how she is ever going to get over this."

As if to compound Margaret's aggrieved sense of frustration
with the world, most of her older friends had married at the
usual age and were no longer gaily single, but had new responsibilities. The Elliotts, the Tennants, the Bonham-Carters and others
had given up gallivanting nightly around London. But a Princess
is never short of company, unless she wishes to be, and a new
"Margaret Set" began to develop in the late '50's.

One of its more prominent members was Lady Elizabeth
Cavendish, a gay, entertaining woman whose company Margaret

came to enjoy and whose advice she came to respect. Elizabeth Cavendish had friends and contacts outside the normal bounds of Margaret's circle: showpeople, actors, painters and photographers. She used this unorthodox, extrovert section of society to breathe new interest into Margaret's despondent life. Elizabeth Cavendish was not prepared simply to be a Lady in Waiting, accompanying her young mistress at a respectful distance, holding her handbag, and looking after the bouquets. She insisted rather on taking the initiative, on flattering Margaret by asking her opinions of various projects, for instance. Instead of making up a *formal* Royal party to go to the theatre, for example, she would take Margaret to a dress rehearsal of a show like *Cranks*, and take her backstage afterwards.

Lady Elizabeth Cavendish recognised, probably before anybody else, the possibility that Margaret would hit it off with the personable Tony Armstrong-Jones. But playing Cupid to Royalty is not an easy business, and few suitable occasions presented themselves for bringing together two people from such widely different circles. After they had been formally introduced in February 1957, they met on a few occasions over the next year— such as at the specially arranged ante-view of Tony's Kodak House Exhibition at his Pimlico Road studio. Like Elizabeth Cavendish, Tony courted Margaret's interest by asking her for her criticism of his past work and her advice on his future projects.

The studio in the ex-ironmonger's shop was strange enough to Margaret, but how much more bizarre was Tony's concept for the 1957 Christmas issue of *Vogue*. He planned a modern Cinderella scenario, set in the kitchen of the Cavendish Hotel, with a bubble-car as the coach that turns into a pumpkin, and the fairy godmother waving a frying pan decorated with sparklers. Margaret was amused.

Tony was exploring new fields. Margaret knew that he was designing the scenery and sets for a second Cranks revue, *Keep Your Hair On*, which was due to open on 13 February 1958. As in his Kodak House Exhibition, Tony planned to dazzle his audience with a series of enormously blown up photographs of ordinary subjects shot from peculiar angles, such as a strutting pigeon's view of Trafalgar Square, or a ten-foot enlargement of a be-ribboned plait of hair.

Margaret never went to see *Keep Your Hair On.* On the opening night it was booed off the stage, the press were universally hostile to Tony's designs, and the revue was taken off after only fourteen days. On that opening night, the boos from the gallery were so loud that the cast could not hear the orchestra, and Tony Armstrong-Jones suddenly paled and rushed to the nearest toilet where he retched violently and loudly for some time.

A few days later, the Alfred Hitchcock thriller *Witness For the Prosecution* was playing at the Metropole Cinema near Buckingham Palace, and Margaret and Elizabeth Cavendish had already booked a bloc of seats to accommodate a royal party. Tony was one of that party. After the film, the group went back to Clarence House, and Margaret found Tony determined not to let the depressing failure of *Keep Your Hair On* affect him too much. Indeed, she found him excited about a new book that he was working on: a photographic documentary of London. Tony had conceived a one-man's view of the city, and he asked Margaret for her opinion both of the idea and of specific photographs. She was delighted. Tony, however, had omitted to bring the photographs with him to Clarence House that evening, and he suggested that the Princess might like to examine them at her leisure over drinks one evening at his discreet Thames-side hideaway at 59 Rotherhithe Street.

So it was that on a March evening in 1958, a muffled, inconspicuously clothed Margaret accompanied by Elizabeth Cavendish took the ferry across the Thames, to be met by Tony Armstrong-Jones and driven to his chicly ramshackle rooms overlooking the river.

This discovery of Rotherhithe excited and amused Margaret more than Elizabeth Cavendish had expected. There was a vague air of adventure in such a visit: travelling incognito across London to rendezvous with a witty and successful young photographer in his bohemian surroundings. It was a heady experience for Margaret, and at the same time the visit was a glimpse of a world where she could find *perfect* privacy, not in the corridors of

Clarence House bustling with family and servants, nor in the showpiece setting of Windsor, but in a tiny, homely, doll's house in a cul-de-sac with the river romantically swirling by. And the young man who had made all of this possible for her could be trusted not to spoil the dream. Tony Armstrong-Jones was totally discreet.

This same March Peter Townsend returned from his world tour. After a brief stop-over in Brussels, he flew to London, and on March 26 he had tea at Clarence House with the Queen Mother and Margaret. His feelings for her had not changed. Margaret, who was only just getting over the long period of depression and illness that had followed their separation two years ago, was no longer so certain. While Townsend remained in London, hoping to see more of her, Margaret flew off three weeks later on a 21-day tour of Trinidad and the Caribbean with Lady Elizabeth Cavendish.

On her return in the middle of May, she found waiting at Clarence House a bulky package initialled T. A-J. Inside was a carefully prepared compendium of the work that Tony Armstrong-Jones had been doing since they last met: the layouts for his London book, designed by Mark Boxer of *Queen* magazine, his latest *Vogue* fashion pictures, a series of publicity shots of Peter Sellers, and some front-of-the-house photographs of *Irma La Douce* and *Auntie Mame*, with a brief explanatory note from Tony himself. It was the first of several envelopes and packages that were to arrive at Clarence House over the next few months, all bearing the tastefully designed monogram T. A-J.

Also waiting in London, hanging on an invitation to Clarence House, was Peter Townsend. His presence in London did not escape the attention of the press. On May 21, the *Daily Telegraph* reported: "Group Captain Peter Townsend visited Clarence House last night for the third time since he completed his round the world tour. He arrived at about six o'clock soon after Princess Margaret returned from the annual meeting of the Student Nurses' Association, of which she is president, and left at midnight."

Rumours once again began to spread about Margaret's romance with the 43-year-old Group Captain, but the Queen, who had approved his visits to Clarence House, put out a statement the very next day after a report of an impending engagement had been carried by a continental newspaper. The statement read: "The Press Secretary to the Queen is authorised to say that the report in the *Tribune de Genève* concerning a possible engagement between the Princess Margaret and Group Capt. Peter Townsend is entirely untrue. Her Royal Highness's statement of 1955 remains unaltered."

Peter Townsend was told to go back to Brussels, which he duly did. And Tony Armstrong-Jones set about strengthening the links between himself and the Princess. His discretion was, still, wholly admirable. Even though he was now seeing more and more of Margaret—through mutual friends like the Hicks in Essex—the press had him virtually married to Jacqui Chan.

Before Margaret's official visit to Canada in July, Tony sought the Princess's advice once more. He was designing a series of "British" ski-clothes (as opposed to French, Swiss or Italian ski-clothes) which would be "fun" and "vividly adventurous." The Princess enthused.

Margaret and Tony wrote to one another during the month that she and Elizabeth Cavendish were in Canada. The tour was meticulously organised, even to finding Margaret perfect dancing partners. Seven Canadian bachelors were "selected, briefed and rehearsed weeks beforehand," each one of them practising with a partner, "the same weight (100 lb.) and height (5 ft.) as Her Royal Highness." For the first time in years, Margaret pulled off an official function with notable success. She was certainly more vivacious, friendly and good-spirited than anyone had expected— and the Canadians responded. In Quebec she was wolf-whistled, and the Mayor of Montreal said of her reception in his city, "I have never seen anything like it." The concern that her family and friends had felt for her health for the past year eased considerably. Any remaining doubts that Peter Townsend might continue to upset her were finally dispelled when after breaking off her Birkhall summer holiday to visit Brussels, she returned after only a couple of days and told her family that she would never see Peter Townsend again.

Tony Armstrong-Jones' career, meanwhile, percolated. In October he managed to photograph a unique scene: Prime Minister Harold MacMillan watching the election results on television at 10 Downing Street, a scoop which Tony claimed to have achieved "by badgering, not by using influence." Later that same month, his ski-clothing show opened at Kiki Byrne's boutique in Chelsea. Lady Elizabeth Cavendish sat next to Tony, and commiserated with him when the showing was a failure and the press lambasted Tony's designs. But the following month he published two very successful books of photographs, one on Malta (with Sacheverell Sitwell), and the other on London, which he had earlier consulted Margaret about. Later that November he left for New York, on an extended fashion photographic assignment for *Vogue*. He stayed there two months and wrote regular, enthusiastic letters to Margaret at Clarence House.

On his return in January 1959, the Queen Mother invited him to tea at the Royal Lodge, and she and Margaret heard his stories of the United States first hand in the elegant sitting room. Margaret, inspired by the anecdotes, rose from her chair and put the record of *West Side Story* on the gramophone. She had recently been to the charity premiere of the film and was as fascinated by it as she was to be fascinated by a host of other musicals over the years. A few days later, she took her sister, Elizabeth Cavendish, Tony, and several others to see the film at a public cinema. The Queen Mother, delighted by this improvement in her daughter's mood, quite rightly attributed it to her growing attachment to the young photographer. Other members of the Royal Family, as they were later to make clear, were not so sure about Tony Armstrong-Jones, but the Queen Mother gave him every encouragement.

Tony, for his part, continued to charm Margaret with his unorthodox courtship. In February, for example, while Margaret was visiting the Nevills at Uckfield, Tony suddenly roared into the estate astride a motorcycle, and screeched to a halt. He had been visiting his grandmother's house nearby and had taken the opportunity to snatch a few hours with the delighted Margaret.

But Tony also had subtlety as a suitor. To impress on Margaret that she was not the only female interest in his life, he flew off in March for an exotic holiday in Davos with Jacqui Chan.

80

Margaret, temporarily disconcerted by this, decided on the spur of the moment to accompany her mother on a visit to Italy. It was by now apparent, both to her family and her friends, that Margaret had more than an ordinary interest in Tony Armstrong-Jones. In Rome, she confided in her old friend Judy Montagu how strongly she felt about him and received her warmest encouragement and best wishes. Judy Montagu was also told of the importance of keeping Margaret's confidences to herself, away from the totally unsuspecting press.

After their return to England, the Queen Mother invited Tony to Royal Lodge, Windsor, and asked him to take the official

Margaret on her 29th birthday, as photographed by Antony Armstrong-Jones

photographs of Margaret for release on her twenty-ninth birthday in August. He took infinite care over this session, taking the informal style that he had introduced to Royal photography to fresh heights. He posed Margaret in a series of carefully composed studies: tinkling carelessly on a piano, looking superbly attractive in a pearl necklace, and gazing pensively over an antique rocking-horse. Tony made no secret of the fact that one of the shots he carried everywhere with him. The relationship which Elizabeth Cavendish had engineered two years earlier was no longer a casual, happy-go-lucky friendship. Friends who invited Margaret and Tony to dinner began to find pretexts for leaving them alone together. On May 26, they went to see *West Side Story* yet again; this was Margaret's fourth viewing. And a week later they had a private showing of the then-banned Marlon Brando film, *The Wild Ones,* at Clarence House. A friend later recalled, "Like other couples, they held hands in the pictures."

The press, all this time, had not an inkling that the relationship between Tony and the Princess was anything more than the relationship between a photographer and his sitter. Exactly what lengths the Royal Family went to to protect Margaret from the kind of press scrutiny that had upset her so much earlier in the fifties, will probably never be known. But a series of deft smoke-screens were arranged. In public with Tony and others, Margaret would sit beside Dominic Elliott or another old friend. Tony and Margaret, extraordinarily, were never photographed together. And in June 1959, the Queen Mother appointed Major John Griffin as press officer at Clarence House to deal with any enquiries about herself or Princess Margaret. Part of his brief was that no information should be volunteered about the romance between Tony and Margaret.

During July, the Rotherhithe retreat was frequently in use. Ironically, since it was owned by a journalist, it played a major part in keeping this royal liaison out of the public eye. Meanwhile in Canada, the Queen took soundings from the Canadian Premier, John Diefenbaker, about Commonwealth reactions to a commoner like Tony Armstrong-Jones. Like her husband and, indeed, most other members of her immediate family with the singular exception of the Queen Mother, Elizabeth had some doubts about the course that her sister was pursuing. There was a general impression in royal circles, an impression that grew with the months and years, that Tony Armstrong-Jones was not *quite* one of them, not quite suited to a position so close to the throne. He was obviously ambitious, even *pushy*, and it seemed hardly likely that he would be prepared to give up his career and knuckle under Royal protocol. Nevertheless, the Royal Family had become increasingly aware that it had over-reacted in its brutal suppression of Margaret's love affair with Peter Townsend, and they were reluctant to make the same mistake again. So, for the first time, Tony was invited to a family gathering, the Royal house party at Balmoral on August 21 to celebrate Princess Margaret's twenty-ninth birthday.

Tony was intelligent enough to know that the family might have doubts about his suitability. He decided that the time had come to wind down his photographic activities. In September, he told Penelope Gilliatt that his current assignment to photograph a *Vogue* cover would be his last for the magazine. When friends asked him about his future plans, Tony was vague, non-committal, and secretive. He made it clear to the Royal Family that he was prepared to sacrifice his career for the sake of Margaret. In doing so he managed to calm some of the fears that Elizabeth and Philip had about the kind of life he would lead as Margaret's husband.

The Queen Mother had no fears. She approved of Tony wholeheartedly and showed her pleasure with her daughter's choice by throwing an extravagant party at the end of October 1959 at Clarence House. The party, at which 250 guests danced to Ray Ellington's Band until 3 A.M., was ostensibly a welcome-home ball for Princess Alexandra, who had been in Australia. But in reality it was for Tony and Margaret, who "positively bounced with excitement." In the early hours of the morning knowledgeable guests exchanged nudges and winks as the Queen Mother persuaded her younger daughter and Tony to lead a massive conga up and down the stairs of that stately old home.

Tony spent Christmas with his sister and the New Year with his mother in Ireland, before joining Margaret and the rest of the Royal Family at Sandringham in January. He had succeeded in satisfying Margaret's family that his expressed intention to give up photography after marriage was genuine. This was of great importance. Tony Armstrong-Jones was largely known as a society and court photographer, and the Royal Family was naturally hyper-sensitive to any suggestion that one of its members should use his position to advance a career. It was consequently vital, they stressed, that he give up photography, and Tony acquiesced. But he could not see himself remaining idle indefinitely, he had not been schooled in aristocratic loafing, and he hardly regarded Royal duties as creative work. So in February he talked to Huw Weldon at the BBC about the possibility of working on cultural programmes such as *Monitor*. Tony was keeping his options as open as possible.

The announcement of the engagement was imminent. The Queen had agreed that it should come seven days after the birth of her third child, which was expected in the middle of February. Tony's father, Ronald Armstrong-Jones, presented them with one of the few remaining problems. Divorced from Carol Coombe, he had been living in Bermuda with a former air-hostess called Jennifer Unite, who was 30 years his junior. He did not wish to attach any scandal to the forthcoming occasion by living openly in sin, so on February 11, at Kensington Registry Office, Ronald Armstrong-Jones did the decent thing and made an honest woman of Miss Unite.

On February 19, the Queen was safely delivered of a baby boy, Andrew. And on the twenty-sixth, an astonished press received the following Court Circular from Clarence House: "It is with the greatest pleasure that Queen Elizabeth the Queen Mother announces the betrothal of her beloved daughter the Princess Margaret to Mr. Antony Charles Robert Armstrong-Jones, son of Mr. R.O.L. Armstrong-Jones, QC, and the Countess of Rosse, to which union the Queen has gladly given her consent."

The Queen Mother, Tony and Margaret were at the Royal Lodge when the news broke and were delighted that their many months of secrecy had been successful. After a couple of days, Tony moved into an apartment in Buckingham Palace, and the frantic world press was left attempting to piece together a story that it had never even suspected. Commander Colville, the

Buckingham Palace press secretary, was not particularly helpful. He told them that the Queen and Prince Philip were "delighted, because this is such an obviously happy match." Others were more forthcoming. Billy Wallace, who claimed to have known about it for some time, said, "This is splendid. I have never known two people better suited to one another. I think it is terribly satisfactory that Princess Margaret and a few of her friends have managed to keep the secret . . . I am overjoyed at the happiness which has come into her life." Sharman Douglas, over the telephone from her Hollywood winter home, said, "I am so excited about the news I can't talk. I cried with joy this morning when I got a telegram from London."

The only person who seemed to have any qualms at the time was Ronald Armstrong-Jones. He confided his many doubts to a friend, and referred to Tony's isolation in Buckingham Palace as being "almost confined to barracks . . . Tony will be in an awful state shut up behind Palace walls, unable to see his friends . . . It's not going to be easy for Tony, you know. I don't like it. His life is photography. I don't know what he will do if he can't carry on with his career. He's got to fight for his independence. He's not cut out for simply being the husband to a Royal Princess."

Ronald Armstrong-Jones' concern about the changes that Tony was going to be obliged to make in his private life was echoed by Mark Boxer, who ruefully commented that certain people in future would "not drop in quite so casually for breakfast."

The public, however, were delighted with the fairytale match. It was somehow perfect that this "gay," "vivacious" Princess should, after her tragic early affair, find happiness with a charming, talented, young commoner. And when the news came out that Tony had refused an earldom before marriage, his stock rose higher, as all doubts about his being a possible "social climber" were removed . . .

The couple was received rapturously whenever they appeared in public, notably at Covent Garden and at Newbury Races. A series of photographs of them together at Royal Lodge were devoured by the press, and everything once more seemed to be moving as planned. Details of the wedding, announced for May 6, were chronicled at great length in the media—what the dress would be like, the cake design, the pageantry of the ceremony in Westminster Abbey—the only point that wasn't settled was the name of the best man. On March 19, it was announced that an old friend would take that role. He was a 35-year-old member of a wealthy family who had known Tony for many years. He owned a delightful 18th century country house near Bath, where Tony and Margaret had spent several weekends. They asked him to be best man on one such weekend—that of March 11—and he was delighted to accept. Before the wedding, he decided to take a brief skiing holiday in Switzerland.

In his absence, Buckingham Palace requested the standard check on his past. To their chagrin, they discovered that he was not a suitable candidate. In fact, he had a criminal record. In 1952, he had been discovered soliciting another man in a public toilet, and at Marlborough Street Magistrates Court he had pleaded guilty and been fined. He had apologised to the magistrate for his indiscretion, explaining, "I am afraid I was rather drunk."

He was summoned back from Switzerland immediately. In reply to questions, he said, "As far as I know, I am still officiating as best man." Four days later it was announced that he had jaundice and would be unable to attend the wedding. His wife said that he had gone on holiday when he had felt the symptoms, in the hope that he would be cured. The press, however, continued to call, and the would-be best man soon delegated the job of answering the telephone to a friend. According to this friend, he soon "got fed up, took his jaundice pills dutifully, and disappeared." In fact, on returning from Switzerland, he had denied reports that he had been ill. All Clarence House had to say on the matter was: "It is not possible to say who will replace him as best man."

All of the newspapers *knew* the actual reasons for the withdrawal of the best man, but not one of them printed them—except for one popular Sunday paper that hinted, "Illness was not, however, the main reason."

On April 11, it was announced that the breach would be

(top) Under the eyes of his new relatives, Tony escorts his wife out of West-minster Abbey (bottom) Honeymooning in Antigua

filled by Dr. Roger Gilliatt, husband of *Vogue's* editor Penelope Gilliatt. Gilliatt was slightly surprised by the request—he barely knew Tony and had only recently been introduced to Margaret—but he was happy to oblige.

One further obstacle stood in the way of a perfect wedding. This was Tony's father's desire to have his new wife beside him during the ceremony at the Abbey. The Palace put an absolute veto on this, and insisted that the Countess of Rosse, also unaccompanied by her new husband, should stand beside Ronald Armstrong-Jones during the wedding, though they had barely seen each other since their divorce in 1935. With that slight embarrassment removed, nothing remained that could flaw this grand occasion.

And grand it truly was. Two thousand guests were invited to the Abbey, the BBC gave a three-hour coverage of the occasion from start to finish, for a world-wide audience of 300 million. Crowds lined the streets, and repeated chants of "WE WANT MARGARET" and "WE WANT THE BRIDE" greeted the appearance of the married couple on the balcony of Buckingham Palace with roars of approval. The car taking them to the royal yacht *Britannia* was many times delayed by crowds who broke through police cordons. The yacht eventually sailed from Tower Pier at 5:33 P.M., its destination the Caribbean.

After the pressures, traumas and protocol of the last few months, the couple found those warm and comfortable islands idyllic. There were one or two public receptions—in Trinidad, Antigua and Dominica—but the couple were able to spend most of their time in private. Margaret said later, "It was so very wonderful for us both, just to lie on those deserted beaches, without a soul in sight." Margaret's old friend Colin Tennant took the opportunity of their honeymoon to show them over his small island of Mustique, drawing their special attention to a 6-acre plot on the southern-most point of the island, describing it as "something we hope you'll accept as a wedding gift." Tony never saw that plot of land again, but it was later to play a crucial part in Margaret's life.

They returned to England in June, and in July moved into their "grace-and-favour" (rent-free) house at 10 Kensington Palace. This was a smallish residence by royal standards, and it was never intended as anything other than a temporary residence, but nevertheless, they were expected to run the household with suitable pomp and decorum. So Lord Adam Gordon, the comptroller at Clarence House, selected a staff including a cook, a footman, a valet, three daily charwomen, and a butler. These joined four official members of the household staff: Major Leigh, Margaret's personal comptroller, her chief Lady-in-Waiting, Iris Peake (who had lately replaced Elizabeth Cavendish), her dresser, Mrs. Gordon, and her personal detective, Det. Inspector Crockett. Tony's secretary from his Pimlico Road studio, Mrs. Everard, also had an office at Kensington Palace—a sure indication that Tony had not *entirely* abandoned his career.

Immediately, there was tension in the household. The new butler, a fastidious and self-important man named Thomas Cronin who had previously worked for the American Ambassador, irritated two other members of the staff. He forbade Mrs. Gordon from eating anywhere other than the servants' table, when she expressed a preference for meals in her room. And he asked Det. Inspector Crockett to refrain from pressing his trousers in the kitchen, saying that if that precedent were set "any old Tom, Dick and Harry" would attempt to take such a liberty.

In most other households of the English aristocracy like those in which Cronin had learned his trade over thirty years, such arrogant insistence on propriety by the butler would have been at least tolerated, if not actively encouraged, by the master of the house. But Tony Armstrong-Jones had not been schooled in such niceties and was stubbornly unwilling to learn them now. He also genuinely considered himself to be a "modern" young man, and all that Cronin stood for was to him anachronistic, wasteful and distastefully irrelevant. On top of this Cronin seemed to be usurping what Tony considered to be areas of his own rightful authority—something Tony was particularly sensitive about, given his inferior social status compared to his wife.

So Tony and Cronin clashed. There were series of running battles, over such matters as Cronin stocking the wine cellar without consulting his master, which led to Tony confiscating the keys; or how much money should be kept in the back-door cashbox for "gratuities and incidental payments"; or Tony's insistence that Cronin should knock before entering the drawing-room— "Sir," Cronin replied, "My training requires me to knock only on a bedroom door"; and even that Tony wore a plum-coloured waistcoat with his dress-suit at a formal tea-party at Buckingham Palace. As a result, Cronin left after only 25 days, in an atmosphere of some acrimony. He was later obliged to deny reports that Tony had given him a black eye.

Nor was this the end of the matter. Cronin was wooed by the popular press and within a month highly unfavourable accounts of life at Kensington Palace had appeared both in the *Daily Express* and in *The People*. And even with Cronin gone, there was domestic strife. Nine days after the butler's departure Tony's valet, Bernard McBride, resigned and returned to the employ of Lord Roseberry. Shortly afterwards one of Margaret's former footmen, David Payne, sold his story to the press. These incidents led to the Royal Family strictly enforcing a clause in their servants' contracts which forbade them from ever writing about their experiences inside the Royal household.

But for Tony and Margaret, such troubles were minor annoyances in what were relatively happy months. Although significantly most of the Royal Family ignored them (Elizabeth visited once that autumn, without Philip, and the Queen Mother called in to jolly things along, but Princess Alexandra, who lived next door, never paid a visit), they often had friends around for informal meals after the theatre, which Margaret and Tony would cook themselves. They continued to pay regular visits to Rother-hithe, taking hampers of food and wine and spending romantic evenings by the dirty old river. They did not appear very much in public, although some joker attempted to rectify this by removing the wax effigy of Tony Armstrong-Jones from Madame Tussaud's and placing it in a public 'phone box.

Tensions between the Joneses and the Royal Family were not, however, decreasing. Their doubts about Tony were exacerbated by his reluctance to join in the shoots at such venues as Sandringham, and when the couple visited Balmoral for Margaret's birthday in August 1960, certain members of the family made their dislike of her husband clear. "Jones," muttered one duke, "Jones! Came to stay with us once. Couldn't stand the fellow. Very, very strange."

In particular, it was apparent that Prince Philip's earlier coolness towards Tony had developed into an active dislike. One close friend explained this: "Their backgrounds, their images, and their private interests are totally irreconcilable. Tony is sensitive, artistic and avant-garde in his outlook. Philip is a model example of the virile, outdoor traditionalist. Tony hates riding and is developing an absolute loathing for shooting."

Tony, quite simply, did not fit in with the Royal Family, who are, as another friend explained, "essentially energetic and sporting folk who love to get up early on their Balmoral holidays, dress in thick clothes and boots, and go out on to the moors for a day's shooting." He found great difficulty in adjusting to the early morning starts and huge breakfasts. Prince Philip and his shooting companions would be in the Land Rover, eager to be away, and Tony would frequently keep them waiting. One morning, after beeping the horn several times, Philip turned impatiently to one of his guests and said, "Where has that bloody man got to? Still in bed, I suppose."

Tony was a frustrated figure then, striding uncomfortably over the bleak moors in the wake of more enthusiastic, gun-carrying, hearty types; wearing grey flannel trousers rather than the kilts and plus-fours preferred by the rest of the family. This was not the kind of life that Antony Armstrong-Jones had envisaged for himself. And the press, recognising his discomfiture, was by the end of the year speculating about what he was going to do, now that it was quite clear that he was not prepared to fit in with the traditional routine of the Royal Family.

The many headlines asked more or less the same question: "TONY—THE BIG JOB PROBLEM" and "WHAT DOES THE FUTURE HOLD FOR MR. ARMSTRONG-JONES?" The stories beneath these headlines were mostly benign, suggesting more that Tony's talents were being under-used than that he was being in any way *lazy*. But they all came to the same conclusion: that he must soon break out of the Royal strait-jacket and re-establish himself in some professional capacity.

To begin with, he took a series of token advisory appointments at the Royal Academy of Dramatic Art, and at the Council for Industrial Design, for instance. And he made the occasional half-hearted official public appearance with Margaret. But Tony Armstrong-Jones was accustomed to the excitement and stimulus of doing a job that interested and stretched him—preferably photographic work—and that he was prevented from so doing by people who had no real empathy with his busy, creative mind placed a burden on his young marriage. Tony was frustrated, and Margaret could not understand his frustration. Their first anniversary, spent at the Royal Lodge with the Queen Mother, was consequently not the most ebullient of occasions, despite the fact that Margaret was by then three months pregnant.

Tony had actually already begun to take steps to satisfy his creative impulses. He had designed a strikingly original and controversial aviary for the London Zoo, and in April the press had taken a great interest in his projected dseigns. Tony had once again been in the headlines in his own right, not just as the husband of Princess Margaret, and he enjoyed the feeling.

By the summer of 1961, various continental magazines and newspapers were printing stories of a rift between Margaret and her husband. *Oggi, France Dimanche* and *Noir et Blanc* wrote that "all is not well between Margaret and Tony," and suggested that certain pressures were pulling them apart.

On October 3, Antony Armstrong-Jones accepted the peerage that he had refused before his marriage, and became the Earl of Snowdon. Despite much talk of his changing his mind in order to cast "a mantle of nobility" over his children (Viscount Linley was born exactly a month later), it must be made clear that Tony's earldom benefited nobody but himself. The children would have inherited titles even if Margaret had been given a courtesy title, such as Duchess, and Tony could have remained a commoner. The truth would seem to be that Tony had hankered after a title all along, and the imminent birth of his first child merely provided him with the excuse to accept one. Tony's family, in particular his mother, were delighted.

If Tony's family was pleased with him, Margaret's—even despite the birth of her son—was less than happy with her. While Tony's sullen reluctance to join in their pursuits annoyed them,

Margaret's behaviour had begun actively to irritate them. For one thing, she made a lot of noise. At Buckingham Palace it was said: "You always know when the Princess is paying a visit—you can hear her all over the Royal Suite." And: "She sings when she plays the piano. She sings to the accompaniment of her record player. She sings when she washes her dogs. And she sings in the bath. Every evening as she bathes before dinner a succession of the latest hit tunes can be heard pouring out from her bathroom. Sometimes her King Charles spaniel, Roly, takes up position outside the bathroom door and joins in the high notes to make it a royal duet."

Her horrendous chattering was also a cause of constant annoyance to her sister and, more particularly, to Prince Philip. On one occasion, when the family was out shooting at Sandringham, a bored Margaret prattled away as Philip tried to take aim. Exasperated, he turned to her and bellowed: "Margaret, will you be quiet, *please.*" Unabashed, Margaret turned on him and reported: "Oh why don't you put down that horrible gun and forget those silly little birds a moment." Philip was also irritated by Margaret's habit of constantly stopping to touch up her make-up while out on a shoot. "To the Prince's way of thinking," says an observer, "the shooting field is not a boudoir, and the only powder around should be the sort that goes in cartridges."

At the dinner table, there was occasionally unpleasant tension. After watching Margaret's food taken away cold and untouched, course after course, because of her incessant chatter, the Queen once despairingly exclaimed: "Margaret, will you please get on with your meal." Even the Queen Mother now and again lost patience with her younger daughter. At a dinner after a ball, a servant brought a coffee spirit burner too close to Margaret's gown which burst into flames, and there was a momentary panic until they were beaten out. The Queen Mother turned to those nearest her and said, "Nothing to worry about. They only wanted to see if Margaret would burn."

After the baptism of Viscount Linley in December 1961— one of his godmothers was Lady Elizabeth Cavendish—Lord Snowdon and Princess Margaret, leaving their infant child behind them, went on a three-week holiday to the Caribbean. While they were abroad, it was announced that Snowdon was to take up an appointment as "artistic adviser" to the *Sunday Times*. This was no precipitous decision on Snowdon's part, no hasty move. He had in fact cherished the idea of such a job for months. He had never really given up photography at all. Thomas Cronin reports that he would spend most weekday afternoons in the dark room at Kensington Palace even in July 1960, a month after the marriage. All he needed was a suitable outlet.

During 1961, Jocelyn Stevens, the publisher of *Queen* magazine, asked Snowdon's old university friend Mark Boxer to invite Tony to help launch "a high-class, non-profit-making photographic magazine designed to boost British industrial products overseas." Jocelyn Stevens explained: "By editing such a magazine, we thought it would solve Lord Snowdon's dilemma. After all, the job we envisaged for him would boost Britain." Unknown to Jocelyn Stevens, however, Mark Boxer was being offered a substantially higher salary by Lord Thomson's *Sunday Times* to leave Stevens and edit their forthcoming colour supplement. Boxer accepted the latter offer, moved to Thomson House, and took Snowdon with him. Jocelyn Stevens was not pleased with this chicanery. "I think that Mr. Boxer was employed by the Thomson Group," he explained, "partly for his undoubted ability, and partly for the fact that the *Sunday Times* thought he might be capable of obtaining Lord Snowdon's services to their staff . . . Look at it this way, if Lord Snowdon was not Princess Margaret's husband, would he have been offered the *Sunday Times* job? The answer, speaking strictly professionally, must be No. After all, he is a photographer, not an artistic adviser."

Stevens paused, before continuing in a bitter voice, "So it is clear that he got the job because his wife is the Queen's sister. That being so, what is now to stop the Queen Mother, for example, from taking a job with some commercial enterprise?"

Jocelyn Stevens was not alone in his criticism of Tony's new appointment. The press which had previously berated him for his apparent idleness and lack of production, now tore into him for joining "an overt and unmistakable part of the Conservative Establishment" (*Daily Mail*). The *Observer* was particularly piqued that its Sunday rival should employ a member of the

94

Royal Family, and an insignificant little magazine called *Topic* made the unassailable point that, "For the first time ever the Royal Family is being involved in a commercial battle in which its prestige will mean an advantage to one of the protagonists. Presumably the Queen and her advisers understood this when they sanctioned Lord Snowdon's job. But that will not ease the critics' chagrin."

Tony was certainly being paid a lot of money for so ill-defined a job as "artistic adviser." His salary was fixed at £10,000 a year, "with expenses." But it soon became clear what Thomson was paying for. Less than two weeks after Tony took up his appointment at the beginning of February, he obtained an exclusive photographic session with the recently defected Russian ballet dancer Rudolph Nureyev at Covent Garden. There was a storm of protest that other newspaper photographers had not been granted similar access by the General Administrator of Covent Garden, Sir David Webster. Snowdon was to suffer such accusations for many years, until, confident and advanced enough in his profession not to need such boosts, he began to insist that all assignments were to be undertaken anonymously, that his subjects should not be told in advance who was going to take the photographs.

At the time, though, the criticism that he received was damaging. Not only did it aggravate his own relationship with his in-laws, but it led—for the first time since 1955—to Princess Margaret being openly scolded by the press. Her lengthy honeymoon, Caribbean holidays, and general reluctance to fulfill official duties in return for the £15,000 p.a. that she now received from the state brought her under fire. "The Queen," it was reported, "seems to have washed her hands of her sister when it comes to fitting her into the official life of the Royal Family." Matters were not helped by the announcement that the Snowdons were shortly to move into larger quarters at 1a Kensington Palace, quarters which were being renovated especially for them at a cost to the taxpayer of £65,000. This figure was originally to have been £85,000, but the Queen, alarmed by the press response, decided to put £20,000 in herself, as a magnaminous gesture.

So it was that by mid-1962 Queen Elizabeth virtually abandoned hope of using her sister and brother-in-law as constructive, active members of the Royal "Firm." They could obviously not act *exactly* as they might please, and they must still fulfill certain official engagements, but Tony was given the leeway to continue his career, and Margaret to fill her spare time as best she could. The direct result of this was that the couple did not see as much of one another as they would have done were they operating as a normal Royal couple. Their natural inclinations were allowed to dictate their lives for the first time since they'd met. And their natural inclinations were as different as they could be. Tony adopted a busy, extrovert, dashing modern lifestyle. His business hours were full and exciting, his leisure was spent on water-skis and motor-cycles. Margaret initially attempted to involve herself in such pursuits, failed dismally (as the newspapers gleefully recorded, every time she toppled from her skis into the water: "SPLASH! GOES THE PRINCESS AGAIN!"), and retreated into herself.

She enjoyed few of the traditional pleasures of motherhood, and outside of occasional trips into the country looking for a rural retreat, Margaret did not find very much to get interested in. She was even edged out of the traditional female role of decorating the new house by the husband who insisted on overseeing every detail. Once more, Margaret was slipping back into depression. Having been for so long an also-ran to her sister, she now found herself in a similar position to her husband. She smoked more, drank more, neglected herself, and became frumpish and ill-mannered even in public. She was described in the *Daily Mirror* as being "perverse and petulant." Even the royalist *Sunday Express* spoke of "the suspicion that she is being paid rather a lot for doing rather a little." Margaret's friends and relations found themselves, yet again, concerned about her well-being. Only this time, the object of their concern was a married woman, and the cause of her depression was consequently a more delicate issue altogether.

London in the mid-60's was, however, an interesting place to be. *Time* magazine had coined the phrase "Swinging London" to describe a new spirit of youthful vibrance in the social scene. In strictly economic terms, Britain had been growing steadily more egalitarian since the war. The wage packets of the average working family had, in real terms, improved monthly ever since 1950. Thousands of working-class children, better educated than ever before, were given the unprecedented chance to break out of their background and actually make an impression on the national character. The Beatles, Mary Quant, David Bailey, Lionel Bart, and many others formed the nucleus of a new social group of people who had become rich and successful through their talents rather than through inherited wealth.

The film actor Peters Sellers, whom Princess Margaret and Lord Snowdon both knew, helped introduce them to this social milieu. Margaret in particular was thrilled and delighted at this opportunity of being entertained by such a variety of new people. For Tony, who came across such people in the course of his profession, it was less of a thrill. Peter Sellers had recently married the pretty young Swedish actress Britt Ekland and together they hosted a number of outings to newly fashionable nightspots such as Annabels and Scotts of St. James. Margaret became a regular at these rave-ups, and in the booming music, the dim lights, the excitement of celebrated company, the plethora of beautiful young things, Margaret discovered once more—as she had in the late '40's and the late '50's—a taste for extravagant nightlife.

In March 1964, she went unannounced—much to the manager's dismay—to the Hammersmith Odeon to see Ella Fitzgerald; in July, she arrived amid cheers at the premiere of *A Hard Day's Night,* and sat next to the Beatles throughout the film. In these public occasions, Margaret granted a sort of royal patronage to Swinging London. Behind the scenes was a stranger world than most of the public imagined. One of the houses that she visited on many occasions, for example, was that of Cockney songwriter Lionel Bart in Seymour Walk, Chelsea. It was a bizarre establishment, decorated in Hollywood baronial style, in which visitors were entertained by a series of unusual features. The visitors' book was extraordinary enough, not so much for its roll-call of celebrities as for what they had written on it: "FUCKING GOOD TIME! GOOD FUCKING TIME!" one film star, now dead, had inscribed. One of the toilets was designed in the style of a medieval throne-room, complete with steps leading up to the seat. Another was completely covered with expensive mirrors, and was equipped with a peep-hole in the wall adjoining an ante-room, through which visitors would gaze into the toilet. There were also two-way mirrors over the beds in at least one of the sumptuous bedrooms.

Margaret was such a frequent visitor to this extraordinary house that Lionel Bart actually attempted to stop the building of a block of flats that would overlook his garden, on the grounds that it was frequently used by Princess Margaret and the proposed block would be an invasion of her privacy.

During these years in the middle-sixties the marriage began to break down. Given enough freedom to explore their own lives, Margaret and Tony discovered what they were never allowed to discover in the vacuum of their courtship: that they did not have particularly compatible personalities. Tony's compulsion to be *active,* his hatred of "wasted time," led him to spend more time away from his wife than was expected of a husband—particularly a royal one.

Not that they were totally out of each other's company. In September 1963, for example, they holidayed together on the private Greek island of Stavros Niarchos, and in August the following year, they spent three weeks with the Aga Khan in his Sardinian retreat. They still fulfilled official engagements together, and were to be seen socially in London. Nonetheless, the time that they were spending apart by 1965 was enough for them both to be seeking extra-marital relationships.

In February of that year, Tony flew to Switzerland for "a short holiday," with "a friend from his London publishing company." It was stated, absurdly, that Margaret could not accompany him because "while the Queen is out of the country Princess Margaret has to stay in London to sign official documents." The faithful Mrs. Everard added: "Lord Snowdon is having a very quiet holiday." By now, Tony had become extremely friendly with Pamela Colin, of the London staff of *Vogue.* His life had changed in many ways. His father, Ronald, who had not long to live, was watching his own prophecies come true. "It will never work out," he was telling friends. "He will be put in an emotional strait-jacket, and that won't suit Tony . . . In a way I have not been a good example, since I have married three times. Perhaps I didn't give him the stability he needed . . . He's not cut out to marry into the disciplined Royal Family."

Ronald probably never got to voice such fears to Tony himself. Since his marriage, Tony had taken no great trouble to see his father, or any of his family. Carol Coombe, his first stepmother, complained that "Tony and I do not keep in touch. Our lives are so different. I have only met Princess Margaret once." She went on to talk sadly of Tony's second child, which was born on 1 May 1964. "I am coming to London for a visit in a few weeks' time, and I would like to see the baby. But I don't suppose I will." As predicted by Mark Boxer five years previously, Tony had re-arranged his social life.

While Tony consorted with the beautiful 28-year-old Miss Colin, Margaret increasingly enjoyed the company of Peter Sellers. The relationship between them became a minor cause of embarrassment to their friends. At one party in Holland Park, London, a discreet host felt himself obliged to admit Sellers surreptitiously by the back door, rather than have him seen publicly entering with Princess Margaret. Some time later, Sellers' friend and colleague Spike Milligan mischievously had a poem read out to the couple when they were seated together at Ronnie Scott's Jazz Club in Soho. It began: "Wherever you are, wherever you be, Please take your hand off the Princess's knee . . ."

The liaison between Margaret and Sellers was, however, never a furiously passionate one. Both parties were too conscious of the fact that they were each under public scrutiny too much of the time to allow anything serious to develop.

It was a casual flirtation, with nothing more involved. This did not apply to another relationship which the Princess embarked upon, with a young man named Robin Douglas-Home.

Douglas-Home came from an old aristocratic Scottish family, other members of which were the Conservative Prime Minister Alec Douglas-Home, and the successful playwright William Douglas-Home.

Robin was less successful. After a brief spell trying to earn a living by playing a piano in a bar, he turned to writing innocu-

(top left) Margaret and Peter Sellers at a London party in the swinging sixties (top right) The ill-fated Robin Douglas-Home (bottom) The Earl of Snowdon, idiosyncratically dressed, on a Royal holiday at the shooting estate of Birkhall

ous features for popular newspapers. One of these, in the *Daily Express* of 26 April 1965, defended Margaret against criticism—largely imaginary—for "consorting with such 'low' company as Peter Sellers."

He admired Margaret from a distance for some time, and when he finally overcame his nervousness enough to try to get to know her, he was delighted to find Margaret receptive, and prepared to reciprocate his affection. They met quietly and frequently at Kensington Palace, and exchanged letters when apart. These letters were the cause of some worry to Buckingham Palace when, in 1970, they were offered for sale to a New York autograph dealer who, recognising their "highly personal" nature, rejected the offer. They were simply too hot to handle.

The whole relationship, in fact, became too intense. In 1967, Tony, disturbed by the fact that Robin Douglas-Home had recently divorced his wife, broke up a tête-à-tête between Margaret and Douglas-Home when he arrived home at Kensington Palace unexpectedly. Tony ordered Douglas-Home out of the house and insisted that Margaret never see him again.

It is doubtful that Tony appreciated the depth of the young man's feelings for Margaret. And even Douglas-Home's friends did not really believe the agonised Robin when he insisted that he could not go on living without her. The following year he committed suicide at his cottage in Sussex. Empty pill bottles were scattered around his body.

Buckingham Palace became increasingly concerned at the diverging private lives of Margaret and Tony. While the couple were no longer expected to do *too* much in the way of royal chores, it was obvious that they must be seen now and again together and in the service of the Crown. So in 1965, what had been first planned as a private visit to the United States was seized upon by the Queen's advisers and turned into a semi-official tour. Margaret and Tony were to spend three weeks travelling from California to New York, combining private activities with public engagements. No one could have foreseen that this would turn out to be an entirely unsatisfactory mix, pleasing nobody and angering a great many.

The first signs of the tour going wrong were recorded in the

American press. Lacking their British counterpart's sycophancy towards the Royal Family, they were not slow to express their disapproval of Margaret's sullenness, bad temper, public lack of graciousness, and general unwillingness to put herself out. Tony, predictably, was more successful with his "common touch," but the impression still remained that this royal couple was not particularly enjoying itself.

The finale to this ill-fated visit was unfortunate enough. Margaret's old friend from the late '40's, Sharman Douglas, now married and back in Arizona, had organised a massive and glittering charity ball in New York, with the Snowdons as guests of honour amid a shining array of New York high society. The ball itself was not an *obvious* failure. It was an all-night affair, and the breakfasts thoughtfully ordered were eaten and appreciated in the dawn light by most of the guests. But between Sharman and Margaret, all was not well. Margaret left New York vowing never to see or speak to Sharman Douglas again—a promise that she has kept. Why did so long-standing a friendship suddenly collapse? Unfortunately, only Sharman Douglas's version is available. According to her, the ball did not make enough money to pay them for coming and Margaret was furious.

"I still miss her friendship terribly," Sharman says, "and I refuse to say any but the nicest things about her. To me she is still one of the most remarkable women in the world. Every year since that happened I've sent her a Christmas card, which she never answers. Whenever I'm in London, I invite her for cocktails. She never responds. I still think I'll be able to get her friendship back some day."

As if such acrimony between old friends was not enough, on Margaret and Tony's return to Britain, an unprecedented storm of press and parliamentary criticism arose. The notorious anti-monarchist M.P., Willie Hamilton, hit out bitterly at the wasteful expense of the trip. He queried in the House: "When will the Labour Government stop conniving at this kind of extravagant nonsense by this very extravagant young lady?"

Normally, Mr. Hamilton's attacks on the Royal Family sailed over the heads of the Commons. This time, though, he had touched a nerve. The fact that the tour had been both private and public meant that Tony, for example, had spent some time publicising his new book *Private View,* in the course of a visit which, as Mr. Hamilton pointed out, was being paid for by the state. The total expense to the British taxpayer, admitted Chancellor James Callaghan, had been in excess of £30,000. Even the old argument about royal tours promoting good trade and international relations rang somewhat hollow, as the American press had gone out of their way to voice their disappointment with Margaret.

The failure of this tour increased the strain in the relations between the Snowdons and the rest of the Royal Family, and between Margaret and Tony themselves. Margaret's ineptitude as a royal ambassador was reiterated when she became involved in a *faux pas* just three months later. On the 'plane to Hong Kong, where she was going to open British Week and promote British exports (which she had so lamentably failed to do in America), her party discovered a number of Arabian businessmen in the first class section. To make way for the Princess, the Arabs were ignominiously bundled into the economy class seats. Unhappily, these gentlemen turned out to be the Emir Sultan, brother of King Faisal of Saudi Arabia, and his aides. They were on their way home where they would be considering signing a £100,000,000 arms deal with Britain. The contract was severely jeopardized by their churlish treatment by the Royal party. Margaret, it seemed, was becoming more of a liability than an asset to the Royal Firm.

As the sixties went by, even in a purely private capacity Margaret seemed unable to command the enthusiasm and affection that she had roused at the time of her marriage. In an extraordinary incident at the Cannes Film Festival in May 1966, this was brought home to her. When she arrived 40 minutes late to see the British entry, *Modesty Blaise,* she was booed by a portion of the audience. Gradually, the whole auditorium joined in, until the racket was so intense that the background music was completely inaudible. Margaret, according to witnesses, "appeared stunned by the unexpected reception." The British Ambassador, Sir Patrick Reilly, standing by her, "was sternfaced and also obviously shaken." The heckling continued for several minutes, only ceasing when the credits for *Modesty Blaise* flashed on the screen.

At the beginning of 1967, rumours of problems in the marriage, coupled with the undeniable fact that Tony was spending less and less time with his wife, led to the continental press eagerly publishing stories that they were on the verge of a divorce. From New York, Tony felt compelled to deny everything. "It's news to me," he said, "and I would be the first to know." As if to confirm Tony's denial, the Snowdons ostentatiously holidayed together in March. Such shows of togetherness were to be staged after every frenzy of press speculation over the next nine years. Elizabeth had spoken in 1949 about the painful subject of divorce. "When we see around us," the future Queen had said, "the havoc that has been wrought, above all among the children, by the breakup of homes, we can have no doubt that divorce and separation are responsible for some of the darkest evils in our society." Her feelings on the subject had not changed.

In the autumn of 1967, the decay in her sister's marriage manifested itself at Windsor. A family luncheon had been planned: Margaret, Philip and the Queen Mother were already there, waiting for Tony to arrive by motorbike from London. After half an hour, Elizabeth grew anxious: "Do you suppose that he's had an accident on his bike?" Anxiety turned to anger, and she snapped: "Why doesn't he come by car like other people?" After waiting for a full hour, they started the meal without him, fortunately, as Tony never arrived. The whole time, as Margaret later discovered and told her sister, he had been with Pamela Colin.

The Queen was insulted. Margaret had been shown up in front of the family, and they were determined to discipline Tony. A family council was called at Buckingham Palace for 18 December 1967, with the intention of working out some acceptable solution to the problem. While this meeting may have been intended to provide a calm and rational answer to the dilemma, it certainly did not work out that way. Tony sat angrily at the table as Philip suggested that they get a divorce. He knew full well the Queen and her mother's feelings about *that* subject, and could safely allow the suggestion to pass by. He also knew that if his conduct with Pamela Colin was unacceptable, Margaret had been just as reprobate in her relationships with others, not least Robin Douglas-Home. The meeting broke up without a resolution. Tony got up and left the palace, and it was at this point that the Queen suggested rather weakly to the downcast Margaret that "each of you go your own way—but please be quiet about it."

Tony later reinforced his moral victory by taking to the Queen a letter which he had intercepted, from Robin Douglas-Home to Margaret. For the time being, the subject was dropped. Tony was now freer than he had been since his engagement to pursue both his professional career, which now ranged into television documentaries and regular photo-spreads in the *Sunday Times* magazine, and other women—although he continued to be discreet about the latter.

But no amount of discretion could hide from friends the fact that the Snowdon marriage was on the rocks. "They've become impossible to entertain," one London hostess exclaimed. "The hate between them is almost tangible—the cold, insulting looks and the little knife-edged innuendos. A lot of married people don't get on, but at least they have the good taste to stay apart from each other at parties, on opposite sides of the room. But Margaret follows him around like a jealous cat."

Another acquaintance reported being with Tony at a dinner dance when Margaret walked through the door and insisted that her husband dance with her. "Oh, go away, you bore me," said Tony in front of the group of male friends that he was talking to. Later, at Kensington Palace, when Tony was showing some photographs to a friend in his office, Margaret appeared with a cup of coffee, which she promptly tipped over a stack of his negatives. Tony left the house swearing and didn't return for four days or nights.

Margaret could not handle the tension and strain of the crumbling marriage as well as Tony. She put on weight, became frumpy and ill-mannered, and failed to find respite in the bosom of her family. On one occasion Elizabeth the Older Sister annoyed Margaret so much—"My sister is always scolding me"; "She was made out to be the goody-goody one"—that she picked up two of the Queen's famous prize corgis and threw them, one at a time, into the lake in Windsor Park. Margaret laughed at Elizabeth's annoyance as the bedraggled animals paddled back to dry land. At the same time, she became more and more imperious. Acquaintances were increasingly treated to her "acid-drop" expression, and sheer rudeness. When a friend asked, "How is your sister?" Margaret adopted a stern expression and replied flatly: "Do you mean Her Royal Majesty the Queen?" Another friend told of another new habit: "When she feels a telephone call is concluded, she simply hangs up without saying goodbye."

Tony, on the other hand, was steaming ahead with his new career as a television documentary director. Even more remarkable, though, was his success as Constable of Caernarvon Castle for the Investiture of Charles as Prince of Wales. He had been appointed to the Investiture Committee in September 1967, partly because of his Earldom, and partly because it was thought that he would bring the kind of contemporary flair and verve to the ceremony that was necessary for the first Investiture to be televised worldwide. The man at the head of the Committee—as of all Royal Ceremonial Occasions—was the arch-traditional Earl Marshal, the Duke of Norfolk. Two more different individuals could hardly be imagined, and at first it seemed that the clash of personalities would do serious damage to the event. Tony designed some massive flats with television in mind, and Norfolk was horrified at their vulgarity. Tony wanted to wear a catsuit of his own design, and Norfolk archly suggested in front of the press that he "go the whole hog and have a hat like Robin Hood." Tony's sartorial habits had already provoked the staider male members of the aristocracy. He had appeared at a television preview of a programme about Lord Mountbatten at the Imperial War Museum wearing a black velvet Teddy Boy jacket hanging to mid-thigh, black suede shoes, and with his hair "quiffed forward in a gentle blond curl over his forehead." Mountbatten, stunned, had gazed at him in open disbelief. As one observer put it: "He might look divine at a camp Kensington soiree but this, dammit, is the Imperial War Museum, Lambeth Road, London, SE1."

Bizarre as Tony's clothes may have appeared to Norfolk and

106

the traditionalists, his energy and imagination in helping plan the Investiture soon overwhelmed them. They just were not prepared for the boyish enthusiasm that he brought to the task, and the Investiture's success was another victory for Tony.

In November 1966, Tony had started to convert a dilapidated freeholding in Sussex called the Oldhouse. It was to be a combination of country studio and secret hideaway—much as Rotherhithe had been. There was one major difference. Margaret was never to visit it. By the end of 1967, the conversion was completed, and Tony began to entertain a combination of society friends and top models (including Bianca Jagger). The most frequent visitor by the end of the '60's was both a model and a friend: the beautiful daughter of the 3rd Marquis of Reading, Lady Jacqueline Rufus-Isaacs. Jackie, as she was known to all, came closer than any other woman to undermining the discretion of Tony's carefully disguised extra-marital relationships.

Only twenty, she fell head over heels for Tony, and never really understood his insistence on maintaining discretion at all costs. Tony concealed his affair with Jackie by the judicious use of her brother, Anthony. Two or three times a week, Tony would visit Jackie at Anthony's flat, and Anthony would frequently be taken along as a third party to dinner parties or restaurant, in order to divert suspicion.

Jackie, deeply in love with Tony, according to a friend, "believed that their relationship could go on almost indefinitely." But when the American press began to publish stories about their "friendship" early in 1971, Tony told her that it was all over. One of his friends explained, "I don't believe he ever said anything to make her think there could ever be more than friendship between them. We thought he was deeply involved, but he says he was never more than very fond of her. I know he was very upset at the things which happened after the story was published abroad about their relationship." When the stories were published, Jackie telephoned Tony and asked him what she should do. He told her to deny everything, and let the rumours die a natural death. He then ceased to visit her.

In December 1969, however, Tony did not see the necessity

for being over-discreet. After being photographed in what the newspapers described as a "tete-a-tete" with Jackie at a party to launch the *Magic Christian*, he was reported to have behaved extraordinarily at the Royal Family's Christmas dinner at Sandringham. According to one report, he "climaxed the evening by leaping on to the dinner table crying 'And now—it's Tony La Rue,' and commencing a lively strip tease."

During the following year, Margaret began to be seen increasingly with Patrick, the Earl of Lichfield, a good looking fashion photographer, who escorted her around town and to country weekends. Margaret spent very little time that year in the company of her husband. And for the first time since their marriage, Tony did not join the rest of the Royal Family for Christmas at Sandringham. One report stated that the Queen had not spoken to him since his striptease of 1969, and he had lost any real inclination to attend such occasions. A friend explained: "It's just that he finds that traditional gathering a depressing and gloomy bore, and he was happy to miss it for once." So, for Christmas 1970, Tony chose to book himself into the London Clinic to have some piles removed. This was not an urgent or serious operation, and his time there was enlivened by visits from Jacqueline Rufus-Isaacs.

There was now real reason for Buckingham Palace to become deeply concerned about the rotting marriage. If Tony was married to anything by the early 1970's, it was his work. To Donald Zec in the *Daily Mirror*, he went so far as to say: "I am a working photographer, and when I am away on assignments I cannot have anyone hovering around me. It is irrelevant who that person is." And Margaret, who some years ago might have welcomed the opportunity to revive their marriage, was no longer interested in a man whom she had seen to be cold, ambitious, and so entirely self-sufficient. Not that there was much future for her with Lichfield—a fact that she certainly recognised. Apart from anything else, he was second cousin to her—and to the Queen.

The best that Buckingham Palace could hope for was that no ghastly indiscretion be committed by either Margaret or Tony, that they should keep their differences private, and that the press should obtain no *solid* information about the full extent of the breakdown of their marriage. This holding operation was not helped by Princess Margaret's Press Officer, Major John Griffin, who in August 1971, when asked whether Margaret and Tony were still together, replied, "Frankly, I don't know. They haven't told me yet."

5

BREAKDOWN

By the end of 1972, additional strains were being placed upon the already tenuous relationship between Margaret and Snowdon. Previously friends and a cautious press had discussed their failing marriage in terms which suggested that a future reconciliation was, if not likely, at least *possible;* it was now becoming more and more obvious that the difference between their lifestyles was taking them, daily, further apart.

It was now quite clear that Tony Armstrong-Jones was simply not interested in seeing out the rest of his days merely as an adjunct to H.R.H. Princess Margaret, in an endless procession of public engagements and society fixtures, especially now that Prince Charles and Princess Anne had reached the ages at which they could begin to shoulder a portion of the royal burden. In fact, Snowdon's commitment to his career as a globe-trotting photographer-cum-socially-conscious man of many parts, had quite eclipsed any of his half-hearted efforts at being a royal functionary. In an interview on December 9, Anthea Disney of the *Daily Mail* saw fit to emphasise that "He doesn't mention his wife," and questioned him not once about his relationship with the Royal Family. Instead, the talk was all about his forthcoming

exhibition at Olympia, his "gadgets galore," and of his professional future: "Fashion editors are always ringing me up and
saying: 'Tony, darling, we know you love doing these social con-
science things (and of course we think they're marvellous).

"But sweetheart, they're just not us. So do you think you
could go to India and take some beautiful pictures of white
tigers?'"

Once again, Snowdon's mimicry—this time of a fashion editor
—won plaudits. Anthea Disney was bowled over. "He's a natural,"
she decided. "Should have been in vaudeville." Nevertheless, she
impressed upon her readers that Snowdon's indignation at such
heartless frivolity was real. In his own words:

"I find it very hard to explain that nothing on earth would
make me go to a country like India just to take photographs of
white tigers. It's immoral. But if I'm there doing some pictures
of the people and I happen to pass a white tiger, I'll take a picture."

This exhibition of his work over the last fifteen years, which
had been displayed earlier in Cologne, was the most concrete
evidence yet of his catholic interests and widespread ambitions
as a photo-journalist. He had decided to show the collection at
the unlikely venue of the *Daily Mail* Ideal Home Exhibition,
because "I disapprove of frames and a reverent atmosphere. Photography should be in the High Street."

Snowdon had also already signed a contract with the *Daily
Mail* for an unprecedented four-page spread of photographs from
his latest book, *Assignments,* destined to be his best seller yet, to
appear on three successive days in the newspaper.

Margaret, meanwhile, did not begin 1973 on an auspicious
note. The American designer Robert Blackwell included her for
the first time in his annual list of the "ten worst dressed women."
Hurtfully (and anachronistically), he commented that she wore
"the kind of styles that make Londoners grateful for their fog."

Far from being grateful for the English weather, Margaret
had always disliked it. It is not difficult to imagine how unsatisfactory a Christmas she had spent at Sandringham that cold
winter, casting her mind back to the four months she had spent
in sunnier climes in 1972. Only three weeks of that time had been

112

on official business, the rest had been idle, happy months in her beloved Caribbean. Her sister's family, never particularly close, seemed to be growing farther apart, with their enthusiasm over Anne's liaison with Mark Phillips, and Charles' increased efficiency and confidence. These things did not particularly interest Margaret.

In this vaguely lonely vacuum, she found herself neglecting her own family responsibilities to her children—never her strong point at the best of times. In the Michaelmas term of 1972, she had sent the 11-year-old Viscount Linley away as a boarder to Ashdown House School, Sussex. Within a month, Miss Ping, a long-serving and devoted member of the Kensington Palace household staff, left to "take an extended holiday." It was apparent that the Snowdon household was not blessed with the most amicable of relationships between upstairs and downstairs.

Pressure on Margaret to fulfill more public engagements in the coming year paid prompt dividends. Throughout January she was to be seen dutifully appearing at functions like a Sunshine Gala Dancing Matinee at the Theatre Royal, Drury Lane, in aid of the Sunshine Fund for Blind Babies and Young People, and at a Gala Performance at the New London Theatre in aid of the St. John's Ambulance Brigade.

Margaret never pretended to enjoy such functions. Unlike her sister, her mother, and most of the rest of the family, she never even pretended to understand their significance. A friend of Snowdon's explains her attitude towards the tedious aspects of the Royal Firm this way: "Hanoverian. She always says that her job—for which she draws a salary of £35,000 (about $65,000) a year—is to help her sister, the Queen, perform various official functions. But she does very little other than appear at gala theatre openings or dedicate some minor orphanage. When she does appear, she can be so surly. She doesn't help the Queen at all, nor the Crown, nor the whole concept of the British monarchy."

Even her private social life was not without unpleasantness. Margaret found herself early in January at a party face to face for the first time with Lady Jackie Rufus-Isaacs, well known to have been Tony's lover throughout 1970 and '71. A room had been put aside for Margaret to withdraw to; characteristically she declined to do so. One of the men present later described the smouldering encounter: "They sat for two hours less than eighteen inches apart, and never said a word to one another. The Princess studiously ignored Jackie Rufus-Isaacs, 'though she does that to people for any number of reasons. Every time Jackie started speaking, Margaret would speak to someone in a louder tone."

Little wonder then, that Margaret was so much looking forward to her visit in February to Mustique, the Caribbean island which she had frequently described as "the only place in the world where I can truly relax." This tiny island had been bought from the French Government in 1959 by one of Margaret's oldest friends, Colin Tennant, the heir to Lord Glenconner, for £45,000. Tennant promptly divided Mustique into a series of smallhold plots, which he gradually sold as holiday homes to the rich of Europe and America. In 1960, when they visited the island on their honeymoon, Tennant had given Margaret and Snowdon the surprise gift of an undeveloped six-acre plot. Since that honeymoon, Snowdon had avoided Mustique, but Tennant nevertheless provided £30,000 for a private villa to be built on the plot. Snowdon's uncle, Oliver Messel, who is handily based on nearby Barbados, designed the villa; Colin Tennant oversaw its construction.

The villa was by now virtually completed, and this February visit would be the last holiday in Mustique Margaret would spend as Tennant's guest. *Les Jolies Eaux,* as she had decided to name her own hideaway, seemed to promise a future with *some* privacy, and an escape from the rigours of her role in public life.

In order not to arouse too much unkind speculation as to what Margaret was doing with the £35,000 which the taxpayers of Britain paid her every year, she rather clumsily attempted to cloud the purpose of this Caribbean trip. It was announced that she was leaving London to go to the British Virgin Islands on an official visit, celebrating their tercentenary. The only official function she performed, however, was to formally open British Week in Barbados.

As a further concession to possible public criticism, Margaret

114

. . . and entering the ball, the off-duty Princess relaxes in her Caribbean paradise

flew out on February 14 with her private detective and Lady Anne Tennant—Colin's wife and Margaret's long-standing Lady-in-Waiting—on a Tourist Class flight. Sharing the cut-price cabin with her were eighteen members of the British Rifle Team. "It seems a pity that she has to travel Tourist Class," quipped one of them. "Perhaps we should have a whip-round on board."

If the last winter had been a gloomy one for Margaret, this spring holiday turned out to be unexpectedly gay and enjoyable. Not for many years had she been so thoroughly happy. Nigel Dempster, the *Daily Mail's* ubiquitous diarist, a journalist not renowned for handling the British aristocracy with kid gloves, was on Mustique at the time and commented that Margaret "was looking noticeably younger than her 42 years." It certainly seemed that this was a new Margaret, blossoming under the Caribbean sun. She seemed relaxed, willing to enjoy herself, and after one dinner party she even helped with the washing-up! Inhabitants, islanders and fellow holiday-makers soon became used to the unlikely sight of Princess Margaret, sister to the Queen of England, "actually queueing for groceries at the one local store."

She capped this holiday in an entirely unprecedented manner. A "Jump-Up" (the local phrase for an into-the-early-hours rave-up) at the Cotton House Hotel, the only local nightspot, served as her farewell party. Margaret had been an exceptionally pleasant, convivial hostess throughout the evening. "Then at half past midnight," one of the guests later reported, "Colin Tennant grabbed the microphone and announced: 'It's cabaret time. Princess Margaret is going to sing.'

"And blow me if the band, brought over from St. Vincent, didn't strike up and she didn't step up and start singing.

"We all sat there and to our amazement and horror she sang *Walk On By* in this tiny little voice. With hand movements like Frank Sinatra's, she went through the whole thing.

"Princess Margaret is a very good mimic and is particularly good at taking off Harold MacMillan. But that is the limit of her accomplishments. The words of songs she knows. But the *voice!*"

Princess Margaret returned to London at the end of March, and found her husband in active form. For his birthday, which

116

(top) At the "Jump-Up": Margaret with Mustique's owner, Colin Tennant
(bottom) On the beach: Princess Margaret holidaying with friends

she had again missed, Thames Television had presented an *Aquarius* special profile of Snowdon. Immediately after the programme, Thames took a large iced birthday cake to the control room, where Snowdon had watched the profile with his daughter Sarah. Later in the presence of a reporter, Snowdon debated where he should send the cake. Sarah protested: "Can't we have it?" "No," came Snowdon's firm reply, "I want to send it to a hospital." One can hardly imagine the Queen Mother herself making a more gracious gesture in public.

It was obvious, on Margaret's return, that for the sake of royal solidarity she must be seen more frequently both with her family and alone, executing royal duties. These did not prove to be too demanding. The religous rock musical *Godspell* claimed the attention of them both for yet another visit, her third, his second.

But soon, there was a threat of another scandal, this time involving Margaret's relations with another man, Jocelyn Stevens. Early one morning (painfully early for Margaret, who does not normally rise until 11.00 a.m.), she was observed watching the sun rise over Bermondsey Market's plethora of antique stalls and shopping for bargains. The only newspapers to obtain photographs of this dawn patrol were the *Evening Standard* and the *Daily Express*, whose managing director is Jocelyn Stevens, the old socialite friend of Margaret's, whose wife was one of her Ladies-in-Waiting. Then the French magazine *France Dimanche*, in its issue of April 22, dragged Jocelyn Stevens into the plot of a largely fictitious story about Margaret's affairs. It completely misquoted the English satirical magazine *Private Eye*, whose gossip columnist, Grovel, was said to have written that Patrick Lichfield —the Queen's cousin—had confided to him that Margaret was having an affair with Jocelyn Stevens.

France Dimanche suggested that the Queen had insisted that Margaret stop seeing the unfortunate Stevens, because Mme. Stevens was threatening to petition for divorce. There was no truth in any of it.

By May, Margaret and Snowdon were *in fact* drifting apart yet again, and their fulfillment of royal duties suffered. Margaret opened a migraine clinic named for her, and promptly came down with an attack of laryngitis. On May 23, Snowdon, to the delight of friends who had "seen him looking strained" and had worried about his health, entered London's King Edward VII Hospital for Officers for a four-day check-up. Once out of hospital, Snowdon seemed completely to forget any family commitments and threw himself into his newfound role as international television film director. Throughout July he was occupied filming *Happy Being Happy* for ATV with sometime companion Derek Hart. He was already signed up by the BBC to film an episode the following month in *The Explorers* series, about Mary Kingsley in Gabon, central Africa. Margaret was scheduled to visit Germany in October, and then Egypt. *The People* on July 15 commented: "Princess Margaret will soon be saying goodbye to Tony—he is going to the Congo . . . He could be away for all of September —and get back just in time to say goodbye again to Princess Margaret." As it turned out, the autumn was to hold more in store for her than her official schedule indicated . . .

Earlier that summer, she had spent a week on the Tiber island of the recently bereaved American art critic Milton Gendel. She had known Gendel for many years, and after his wife had been found dead in London in November of the previous year, he had stayed with Margaret at Kensington Palace. Margaret spent this week on the Tiber in June accompanied by only her personal detective.

Perhaps the vaguely carping notices in the British press, perhaps the occasionally scandalous items in the European media, perhaps simple Palace pressure made Snowdon and Margaret take a short holiday with their children in Italy during the middle of August. Snowdon spent much of the time sporting a T-shirt with the word LONELINESS printed on it, and smiling. Princess Margaret was less pleased by the persistent attentions of the paparazzi, who caught her in a number of unflattering poses in a swimsuit. It was apparent that she was no longer the trim 7 stone 2 pounds of her early married days.

On August 22, Margaret took the children to Scotland, and two days later, Snowdon left for Gabon. He was there for nearly two months, and it was during this period that Margaret met Roddy Llewellyn.

Jeans and cowboy shirt for the handsome Roddy Llewellyn (Inset) Colonel Harry "Foxhunter" Llewellyn being presented with an award in 1952 by the new Queen of England

Roddy Llewellyn has been described by the gay man-about-town Nicky Haslam as "a lovely, sweet, angelic boy," but this reticent young man had not done very much in his 26 years. The son of Olympic show-jumping champion, Colonel Harry "Fox-hunter" Llewellyn, and the younger brother of the same Dai Llewellyn who had snatched Jackie Rufus-Isaacs away from Snowdon in 1970, Roddy had not found it easy to assert himself. Nicky Haslam, ten years older than Roddy, described Roddy's family this way: "His mother is divine, absolutely divine, very fay. But his father is a very bluff, overbearing man . . . You must understand that Roddy has always been a bit jealous of his brother Dai."

Certainly, Roddy had not enjoyed the same degree of success as had his brother, either at work or with women. While Dai's conquests were spoken of with awe in certain smart London circles, Roddy's were never mentioned. And where Dai had been a moderate success in the City, Roddy had barely been able to hold down a job. The tension between the two brothers had existed since childhood. Dai had followed in his father's footsteps and gone to Eton. Roddy had actually failed the elementary entrance examination. To his family's disappointment he had to be sent to the less prestigious school at Shrewsbury.

But Roddy is, without doubt, an extremely attractive young man. He is five foot ten inches tall, slim, blond and handsome. These qualifications had got him a spell of work in South Africa in 1971 as a male model with the Veronica Summers Agency. Miss Summers, who described Roddy as "a very friendly and charming young man with a few freckles," said that clients "liked him very much and asked for him again."

When Nicky Haslam met him the following year, Roddy was working at an art gallery. "I don't know what he was actually doing," insists Haslam, "doing what people do at galleries, I suppose, selling pictures.

"He wanted to buy a flat in Fulham. Honestly, it was so awful. I said to Roddy, 'You're mad to spend your money on such a flat.'

"It was in one of those funny little back streets. You went up some cramped stairs. Just horrid. I said: 'Look around, don't rush into anything.' So he had nowhere to live. I said: 'Come and stay on the sofa,' and he did."

As a cousin of the Earl of Bessborough, Nicky Haslam was no stranger to Royalty. He had known people like Princess Margaret since childhood: "I sort of came out of the same circle she was in." Such connections secured for Roddy in early 1973 a vaguely defined post as "a research assistant" to Sir Antony Wagner, Herald of the Royal College of Arms. It was while Roddy was working at the Royal College of Arms that he received an invitation to a weekend house party at Glen House, Innerleithen, Peeblesshire, the 18,000 acre Scottish estate of Colin Tennant.

Despite the surface erosion of the old world patina of English upper-class life, many of their outmoded and almost byzantine practices continued well into the 1970's. Colin Tennant's infrequent house parties were oddly anachronistic affairs, reminiscent of the great, untroubled days of the British aristocracy. Close friends of the family would be invited to spend a weekend being cosetted and entertained. For this purpose, amusing and suitable company would be provided.

On the weekend beginning Friday, 14 September 1973, Colin Tennant's principal guest was Princess Margaret. Of the people invited to that weekend's party, one young man had to drop out at the last minute, leaving an imbalance in the sexes present. Roddy Llewellyn's name was mentioned as a suitable candidate to fill the gap, and he consequently received a call. His train fare was paid for, and he immediately left for Edinburgh.

It was customary for Colin Tennant to arrange a meeting between Princess Margaret and the prospective house-guest before actually inviting him up to Glen House. Margaret was not noted for her even temperament, and Tennant didn't want to invite anyone who might be distasteful to her. On Saturday 15th, he introduced her to Roddy Llewellyn over lunch at the Cafe Royal, Edinburgh.

After lunch, Tennant told the young man to expect a telephone call later that day, and Roddy remained in Edinburgh. After getting the call, Roddy travelled the thirty miles to Innerleithen. He was met there by Colin Tennant's Range Rover.

Seated in the car, most unexpectedly, was Princess Margaret, who had travelled from the House to welcome Roddy. The attraction between them was immediate and apparent.

Of this relationship, which resulted in the public collapse of Tony and Margaret's marriage, Lady Anne Tennant—Colin's wife—said: "It was all a mistake. Roddy was meant for another girl—much younger than Margaret. He wasn't intended as Princess Margaret's partner or date or anything like that. Something seemed to happen between them.

"It is quite true that Roddy and the Princess hit it off immediately. I suppose no one knows what qualities people see in each other, but they do seem to make each other happy. I was quite surprised because Roddy was really meant for one of the younger girls. One doesn't actually try to pair young people off, but obviously it is much better to have an even number. That is why he was asked."

Another guest remarked: "Within twenty minutes of meeting, they were nattering away as if they were life-long friends. She is not usually so spontaneous with her friendship."

That first weekend was spent in "picnics and walks." Lady Anne Tennant later recalled: "I remember thinking what a quiet, shy young man Roddy was. He had nothing like the confidence he has now. Their friendship began at the party, but none of us realised how strongly it would develop."

For two months after the party, it would develop in London. Colin Tennant lent Margaret a house in Tite Street, Chelsea, where she met Roddy frequently. Her official visit to Egypt was cancelled on October 16, owing to the Yom Kippur War, and Margaret was left with an unexpected amount of free time to be in Chelsea.

Margaret's lack of popularity in the press and the public eye was as obvious as ever that autumn, a fact which must have made her private life seem even more attractive. The *Sunday Mirror* (Britain's second highest selling Sunday newspaper) on September 16—the very weekend that Margaret first met Roddy—placed her at the bottom of a poll of Popular Royals. Socialist Member of Parliament Willie Hamilton later explained the people's vote by declaring: "She makes no attempt to conceal her expensive, extravagant irrelevance and it is impossible to make out any honest case for her being much use to anybody." On top of that, articles in the popular press continued to make uncomplimentary remarks about her "weight problem."

No wonder, then, that she took refuge in the flattering attentions of this attractive young man. Roddy, for his part, seemed more prepared than most to pander to Margaret's extremely demanding nature. Nigel Dempster explains the rigours of being in her company: "She can be exasperating, and needs to be entertained. It is very tricky having constantly to be on your guard. You've got to be polite and courteous, you can't swear, you can't get drunk. She demands the utmost respect. You've got to call her 'Ma'am' all the time—*everybody*, even her closest friends like Colin Tennant, have to call her 'Ma'am' all the time. Only one or two people, like Patrick Lichfield and Jocelyn Stevens, are allowed to call her 'PM' in private."

Earlier that year, when Dempster had arrived in Mustique, he was greeted by Colin Tennant who said, "Thank God you've come. I've had dinner and lunch with her for thirty-eight different meals in a row, and now someone else can take over."

As the years went by, Margaret had come to expect an extraordinary degree of formality from her friends and acquaintances. The comparatively lively Princess of twenty-five years ago had changed by now into a middle-aged woman who, to quote another friend, ". . . knows exactly who she is. The sister of the Queen of England. And you are never allowed to forget it.

"Everybody calls her 'Ma'am.' It is impossible to be familiar with her. She can say 'my sister' but you aren't allowed to say 'your sister.' You must say 'the Queen.' If you slip and say 'your sister,' she'll look at you and say 'Who?' and you must say, 'I'm terribly sorry, Ma'am. The Queen.'

"To be in her company for very long periods can be boring."

The 26-year-old Roddy, however, elicited a response from Margaret that surprised all of those around them. Perhaps it was his footloose lifestyle, perhaps it was his peculiar air of vulnerability, in addition to his obvious physical charms, that drew Margaret to him. And surprise on the part of their friends was mingled with some relief. As one of these friends put it: "Nobody

124

really finds either of them very amusing, but they make each other laugh. Roddy and Margaret really find each other quite marvellous."

As that autumn drew towards winter, their influence upon each other drew remarks from associates. Margaret became less edgy, slightly more open, and seemed to benefit from the constant presence of this casual young man. Unlike so many of the people in her usual social and official circles, Roddy seemed to be almost devoid of ambition. In contrast to Snowdon—an outgoing, confident, articulate man—Roddy was painfully shy, introverted, and had very little to say for himself. He fitted in perfectly with Margaret's needs to escape the world of twentieth century Royalty and enabled her to relax from its pressures.

In her turn, Margaret gave Roddy the kind of attentions that he had never before received from a woman. She bought him clothes, had his hair styled by her personal hairdresser, took him to expensive restaurants, and entertained him at Kensington Palace in Snowdon's absence. For the first time in his life Roddy was able to regard himself as something better than the failure that his father and brother Dai had always considered him to be. Dai's smart City-set, with their "Mercedes and dolly-birds," had always treated Roddy as a joke. Now somebody a good deal more important than any of Dai's friends was treating him as a serious human being.

For both Margaret and Roddy, it was a heady experience. Margaret, at the age of 43, was on the verge of a grumpy middle age. She had been unable to keep up with the pace set by the ever-trendy Snowdon, and unable to compete with the constant stream of attractive young women who meandered in and out of his life. Roddy Llewellyn allowed her to regain some of the sexual confidence that she lacked for so long. And whether she knew it or not, Margaret was doing the same for him.

Their friends may have remarked upon the relationship, they may have commented about how well the pair "hit it off together," but not one of them understood the liaison sufficiently to appreciate what it was that attracted them to each other. And consequently, not one of their friends could foresee how deep this affair would go, how many years it would last and that it would inexorably destroy the vague understanding that had kept alive the marriage of Margaret and Tony.

At the time, it seemed to be doing nothing but good. Margaret's visit to Germany at the beginning of November was an enormous success. The inhabitants of Munich responded to this smiling Princess by feting her with unusual extravagance. Even *The Times* reported that "officials were surprised at the warmth of the spontaneous welcome accorded to Princess Margaret." Margaret was equally surprised, and not a little delighted by the reception. Two incidents occurred during her stay at the Vier Jahreszeiten Hotel in Munich. Maria Callas, on a come-back tour of West Germany, had booked into the same hotel. On discovering that the entire State Suite on the top floor of the Vier Jahreszeiten had been reserved for Princess Margaret, Callas refused to take a less prestigious suite, cancelled her booking, and moved into the Presidential Suite of the Hilton instead.

The other incident was a telephone call from a flustered and distraught Snowdon, telling her that he had been shaken up by a fall out of an invalid car he had been testing in the grounds of Kensington Palace that afternoon. It is intriguing to speculate at the nature of the official pressure brought to bear on Snowdon to make that call, and tell the press about it. Left to his own devices, Snowdon would certainly not have asked for Margaret's sympathy.

On November 14, Margaret and Snowdon were publicly reunited for the wedding of Princess Anne and Captain Mark Phillips. As Snowdon and Margaret travelled together in their coach to Westminster Abbey, the irony of the situation can hardly have escaped them. This glittering celebration had much in common with their own marriage in 1960. Once more a Princess was marrying a commoner, once more the public's imagination had been fired by the fairytale romance of the match. The cheers that echoed around the procession had once been for them.

Margaret and Snowdon did not stay together after the wedding any longer than was necessary to keep up appearances. Two days later, on the Friday, Snowdon once again entered the King Edward VII Hospital, this time for a minor chest operation. Margaret spent that weekend in the country with "a friend"—a euphemism that was occurring more and more frequently in the press.

Needless to say, she did not visit Snowdon in hospital, and the next week, Margaret left London for Mustique, via Barbados. It was announced that Lord Snowdon "was not planning to go with her." Said a friend of the Earl, "He has been in pain for some time. He will be in hospital for a week or so. I think it is to do with his polio."

Margaret was visiting Mustique in order to take possession of her villa, which had just been completed. She was flying out, as usual, for her own enjoyment, but much play was made of the fact that Anne and Mark would be starting their honeymoon by joining the Royal Yacht Britannia in Barbados, a mere ninety miles from Mustique. It was suggested that they might wish to call in at the island, in which case Margaret was only being hospitable by making sure that she was here to greet them. In fact, Anne and Mark did not visit Mustique, and never had any intention of doing so.

The Georgian-style villa had three bedrooms, an open-plan sitting room, and a permanent staff of three. It overlooked a private bay on the most beautiful and secluded part of the island. Margaret was delighted with her "shangri-la." The arrangement was not only satisfactory to her. As Nigel Dempster confided: "Tennant has got one million pounds of his money stacked into an island on which twenty-eight houses are built. He brought Margaret over there, he gave her some land, he paid out of his own pocket £30,000 to build her a house. He has put her out on a point of the island and says maybe you'll see Princess Margaret, maybe you won't. It costs around £60 a day to stay on Mustique.

"He's been very clever about it, and all power to him. She gets what she wants, he gets what he wants, and he's publicising the island through her.

"But they are very old and close friends. Make no bones about it. And he is quite fond of her. But he is exasperated by her."

Even with the new villa, Margaret's routine varied little from previous years on Mustique. "She invariably breakfasts in bed at about 9.00 a.m. off fruit, toast and marmalade, and a pot of her specially imported Earl Grey. Then at about eleven she appears at the 'watering hole' for morning drinks," one friend who was her guest on the island reported.

"In her hand is the inevitable cigarette in a long tortoise-shell holder. She has been warned that she smokes too much, but she has chain-smoked since she was twenty, and shows no sign of letting up. One of her unusual mannerisms is the way she smokes. She holds her cigarette-holder between thumb and second finger, and uses it like a baton to conduct a conversation or dismiss people.

"The most typical sight of the Princess on holiday is to see her with cigarette-holder in one hand and a glass in the other. She thoroughly enjoys a drink and expects one to be about when she appears in the morning. Of course, she never orders a drink, and would never walk up to a bar for one." The daily ritual rarely changes: "When she appears one says, 'Good morning, Ma'am, I wonder if you would like a drink?' Her reply to this is, 'Oh, you're not drinking are you? But if so, I'll have a G & T.' Gin and tonic is her favourite drink. Normally, she has the first at about eleven, but I have drunk with her two hours earlier than that. Like the cigarettes, the drinks are endless."

After morning drinks, there is lunch either at her house or the hotel. "She informs Colin Tennant in advance if there is anyone on the island of interest whom she would like invited. Colin patiently eats with her at virtually every meal. He must arrange the guests, keep her amused, and keep the undesireables away."

In the afternoon, there is the obligatory half-hour swim. "Princess Margaret always wears very frilly, 1950's style one-piece outfits. Being only five-foot tall, and having a considerable bust, a bikini is out."

Bizarrely, even on holiday she wears incredibly heavy make-up. "Almost like a circus clown with very red lips and her eyes done up to the nines. The rest of her body gets nice and brown— but not her face. She never allows her head to go under water when swimming, and to see her launch herself is quite a sight. When the moment comes she will say 'Now we will go swimming,' and one replies, 'Yes Ma'am.'

128

"She swims for about twenty minutes, then treads water and engages one in conversation. And one is obliged to paddle away and chat back. One hovers there, trying to keep afloat, and there is absolutely no escape whatsoever. Then she decides to swim back and one has to swim alongside or slightly behind, like a sort of flotilla. And behind you both comes the detective, who is always with her. He doesn't often enter the water, but strolls along the beach keeping pace and getting red from the sun."

In the evenings Margaret is frequently to be seen at either the Cotton House Hotel, or at The Hut, a beach restaurant which boasts an open-air dance-floor. "Normally one dances with Margaret at her suggestion, but occasionally, if she is in the right mood, she will agree to dance if one of the other holidaymakers asks her. But far more often she is not in the mood, and the poor would-be partner is treated to one of the 'freeze-outs' for which she is notorious.

"She doesn't say 'No' or 'Get Lost.' She simply ignores the person as though they did not exist. She sits there waving her cigarette-holder and talking to one of the people at her table, and not by a look or a gesture does she acknowledge the newcomer's presence."

In early December, Margaret returned to London and to the waiting Roddy. Snowdon, put out by the lukewarm reviews accorded to *Happy Being Happy*—his latest ATV documentary which was shown on December 10th—was working with increased zest. He had no time to rest, it seemed, as he made perfectly clear to Sheridan Morley in *The Times*. He was determined to do more and more demanding work, to immerse himself in it. There was something fixated in his insistence on the value of achievement. He told Morley: "This year I've had a slightly difficult time with my health, and I've been told not to do too much . . . but then one looks back at the end of a year, even of a whole decade, and thinks 'What on earth have I achieved?' Any waste of time depresses me, like going for a walk. I don't mind walking *to* somewhere, but just going for a walk and ending up back where you started seems to me incredibly futile."

If Snowdon had set out to encapsulate in this interview the immense difference between himself and his wife, he could hardly have done it better. Not surprisingly, they spent the winter apart. Margaret, in between her usual seasonal round of family engagements at Sandringham and elsewhere, was able to see more and more of Roddy. Snowdon enjoyed himself in a variety of different ways. Occasionally, these were somewhat bizarre. As on the night of 13 January 1974, when he was said by locals to have startled the diners at the Vine Eck Restaurant, in the Swiss village of Klosters, by "jumping to his feet during the singing of the Swiss national songs and shouting 'Heil Hitler!' several times," and had to be asked to leave.

In America twelve days later, he was pulled in off the street and detained by Detroit police. He was on an assignment for *The Sunday Times*, doing a feature on "Crime in the U.S." and was photographing two young Detroit cops making an arrest when they took offence. Finding that his credentials were not in order, they decided to take him downtown as well. When they confirmed that he actually was the Earl of Snowdon, he was released.

Snowdon had long been proud of the fact that he worked anonymously, sometimes even in disguise. In New York the following weekend, society columnist Suzy Knickerbocker refused to believe that, as Snowdon said: "I had worked in Detroit unrecognised. I told her I had, and bet her I could do it again. And I won." Snowdon did it by arranging with hostess Mrs. Jane Pickens Langley for himself and his New York agent Peter Schub to pass themselves off as butlers at a party at her Park Avenue apartment. Throughout the evening he ferried trays of drinks and food, wearing clothes borrowed from a Chinese servant, and with his hair plastered down with a middle-parting—twenties style. To add to the illusion he wore his agent's wire-framed glasses. He spoke in what was described as "an adorable French accent." Snowdon was very pleased with himself. "I knew I could pull it off," he said. "I never have trouble making sure people don't recognise me."

Small wonder, then, that he became so angry later that same February when booking into the Athens Hilton incognito, he was recognised and photographed by a Greek pressman. Snowdon complained to the hotel detective, and demanded that the Greek photographer's film be given up to him. The request was refused.

In London, Margaret—buoyant from Roddy's company—was finding even the more tedious of royal tasks bearable. During the petrol crisis she made the public gesture of driving to and from engagements in a modest 25 miles per gallon Vauxhall Victor instead of the usual £11,000 Rolls Royce. And when she flew off to Cyprus for a five day official visit on January 21, it was together with an army troop in an RAF VC10 to conserve fuel. The discomfort may have been tempered for her by the knowledge that she would shortly be returning to Mustique, this time in the company of Roddy Llewellyn. Interestingly, her villa had not been unused in her absence. Among the tenants who had rented it at £400 per week were Rolling Stone Mick Jagger and his wife Bianca, as well as the well-known barrister John Nutting and his new wife, the former Countess Beatty.

"Leasing it is not so surprising really," explained Colin Tennant. "Princess Margaret likes to let it to help defray costs . . . Nobody is really vetted by me before they move in, but we don't advertise." The exclusivity of Mustique was, and is, a precious commodity. Tennant found himself having to guard it even more jealously when Margaret returned for a three-week holiday on March 3rd. This time, she had brought Roddy with her. That would have been risky enough in itself, but the fact that the U.S. magazine *McCalls* was to publish in its April issue a sensational article, the first of its kind, claiming to document the breakdown of Margaret and Snowdon's marriage, made matters much worse.

The article, which had been written some time before, listed a number of incidents substantiating its thesis that Margaret and Tony had for a long time been incompatible. Curiously, most of its information was about events that had taken place four or five years earlier.

The fact that *McCall's* placed so much emphasis on Snowdon's extra-marital affairs, and so much emphasis on Margaret as a tragically misused wife—"The blue eyes now hold a haunted weary look. The heavy make-up that she wears cannot hide the hard and bitter lines that have developed around her mouth"—gave a lopsided impression of the affair.

The article did, however, reflect the unpleasant nature of this royal couple. It retold the story, for example, of how Margaret tossed two of her sister's prize corgis into the lake at Windsor Park. It repeated how, after the dinner-dance at which Snowdon had told Margaret "Oh, go away, you bore me," Margaret had tipped coffee over a stack of her husband's negatives. "As for their marriage, it's perfectly obvious that things are bad, but their behaviour toward each other—well, I hate to use the word, but it's perfectly *common.*"

The publication of such stories for the first time in the English language legitimised the subject for the previously reticent British press, which attempted to make up for lost time with a flurry of front page stories and speculation about divorce. And, for possibly the first time since its institution, the Court P.R. apparatus found itself unable to cope. Reactions from royal circles varied from "Absolute bunk!" to "These things come up regularly," to "This has been a very rough marriage . . . It is well known that for a long time they have agreed to disagree."

The *Daily Mirror,* hoping to collect pictures of Margaret holidaying with Roddy Llewellyn, lost no time in sending a reporter and a cameraman to Mustique from their New York office. For an island where, according to its owner, no visitor was "really vetted," Mustique afforded the *Mirror* journalists a peculiar reception. Their aircraft was refused permission to land on the island's tiny landing strip by a resolute Colin Tennant waving a shotgun.

In such an intense spotlight of press attention, Margaret was obliged to return from Mustique alone on March 27, and Snowdon was obliged to meet her at Heathrow Airport. Enormous play was made in the British newspapers (as happy as ever to print any Royal human interest story, even based on an obviously staged event) of Snowdon's greeting Margaret with a kiss on the cheek and thoughtfully draping a fur coat round her shoulders. The Viscount Linley's presence at the airport completed the "happy family reunion."

In order to forestall any further public comment about the state of their marriage, Margaret and Snowdon resumed the fulfilling of official functions together. And when Snowdon made his maiden speech (breaking thirteen years of silence) in the House of Lords on April 10, on the dangers of "intrinsically lethal" invalid cars, the press dutifully reported that Princess Margaret and their two children watched from the Peeress's West Gallery.

Fortuitiously, the Snowdons were due to leave at the beginning of May on a visit of the U.S. and Canada, giving them the opportunity publicly to refute the *McCall's* article in its land of origin. The Royal Press Office, having got over its earlier embarrassment about the Snowdons' separation, now pulled out all the stops. Photographer Terry O'Neill was commissioned "at the Snowdons' special request" to shoot a set of delightfully relaxed family pictures. These photographs of household togetherness were distributed to, and printed in, most of the British press just a day or two before they left for the Americas.

As soon as they arrived in Kentucky, Snowdon set about refuting the unpleasant rumours in a number of subtle ways. Without saying *anything* about the state of his marriage, he explained their separation thus: "I lead two lives. There are official tours like this, and my own life as a photographer. When I'm working, I naturally don't take the wife and kids along on every job." This piece of non-information was taken by sections of the British press as constituting a denial of the rumours, and of there being any rift in the Snowdons' marriage. One newspaper actually misled its readers by headlining a story based on nothing more than the statement quoted above: "SNOWDON SAYS: I NEVER EVEN CONSIDERED LEAVING MARGARET."

Their American tour was an enormous success. If the U.S. press had expected to be given a glimpse of a royal marriage *obviously* on the rocks, they were disappointed. For a week, Margaret and Snowdon managed to conceal their distaste for one another's company. By the end of their visit, the spectre of divorce had receded sufficiently for them to go up to the 40th floor of the Waldorf Astoria and call on the recently bereaved Duchess of Windsor.

Their visit to America had been successful in quelling public curiosity about the state of their marriage, and Margaret and Snowdon were able to spend the rest of that summer of 1974 pursuing their own separate lives without arousing comment. For Snowdon this meant continuing his photographic career and lining up his first American exhibition. For Margaret, it entailed a series of minor official functions. Very occasionally, they put in an appearance together, but for the largest part of the summer, Margaret was free to resume seeing Roddy.

This relationship was developing, now, on a firmer basis. It was helped by the fact that Roddy had moved into a basement flat in Walham Grove, Fulham (which by ironic coincidence had once been occupied by Snowdon's old friend Bob Bolton). This gave them, for the first time, somewhere to meet discreetly in London, and Margaret chose the decorations for the flat. By the time Snowdon returned from America at the end of October, he had decided to stop tolerating his wife's affair with a man seventeen years her junior. They had arguments throughout November which culminated with Snowdon demanding in December that Margaret stop seeing Roddy, as he had demanded that she stopped seeing Robin Douglas-Home seven years ago.

Snowdon's demands were helped by the timely intervention of Roddy's father shortly before Christmas. Harry Llewellyn had grown increasingly embarrassed and concerned about his younger son's attachment to Princess Margaret, and Roddy was peremptorily packed off on a winter's holiday in Turkey.

It was only after Christmas, when Margaret returned from the family festivities, that she discovered that Roddy had, in effect, been sent away from her. She immediately cancelled a number of engagements and began acting very strangely. Instructions were given to a man at the Embassy in Istanbul to contact Roddy and get him back to London with the offer of "a job in the City." Roddy, who had not been working for the Royal College of Heralds for some time, returned. If there had been a job in the City, there is no evidence that Roddy ever took it up.

Roddy's return was partly responsible for Snowdon's extraordinary outburst against anti-Royalist Labour M.P. Willie Hamilton's critical study of the Royal Family, *My Queen And I*, in January 1975. Snowdon attempted to stop the book being published on the grounds that it contained certain alleged "inaccuracies." These were so trivial as to defy belief. They included

134

the misprinting of his name, an incorrect assertion that he employed a second footman, and inaccurate details about the length of time his personal secretary had been in his service. This was Snowdon in his role as chivalrous champion of defenceless Royalty, perhaps thinking to ingratiate himself with the Queen and her family. It is more likely that Snowdon rationalised his attempted curbing of the relationship between Margaret and Roddy as another instance of his regard for the correctness of the Royal image.

Snowdon left London at the beginning of February for a long working trip in Australia, and Margaret left for her annual holiday in Mustique, this time unaccompanied by Roddy. She was escorted by Dominic Elliot, an old beau, one of the 1950's "Margaret Set," and he did what he could to enliven her holiday. Roddy meanwhile had journeyed to neighbouring Barbados, where his father had a house, on the understanding that Margaret would call him to go on and join her in Mustique. That call never came.

Roddy became increasingly distressed in Barbados, especially when he fell victim to a practical joke which played upon his weeks of frustration and anxiety. He was told that Margaret finally had called and wanted to see him in Mustique. But when he arrived on the island he found her preparing to return to London, and denying all knowledge of having summoned him. Roddy collapsed.

Whatever their feelings for one another at this point in their relationship, a combination of various external circumstances and mutual misunderstandings conspired to keep Roddy and Margaret apart. Roddy's breakdown was in fact so severe as to necessitate his being flown home and admitted to Charing Cross Hospital, where he underwent treatment in the psychiatric ward. Margaret certainly did not intend to put him through all that. And even though she obviously could not visit a friend in the psychiatric ward of a public hospital, she did send him a letter calling him, "My Darling Angel," hoping he would soon be well, and promising to visit him again shortly in the Fulham flat.

Meanwhile, Lord Snowdon was in Australia with his capable new production assistant, Lucy Lindsay-Hogg. Ms. Lindsay-Hogg,

Filming in Australia, Lord Snowdon with his production assistant, Lucy Lindsay-Hogg

30, former wife of Michael Lindsay-Hogg, the director of the Beatles' film *Let It Be,* had been divorced since 1971. She had not merely been seeing Snowdon in a professional capacity. Since 1972 Snowdon had spent an increasing amount of time at the Old House, his Sussex country cottage which Margaret had never visited, and Lucy Lindsay-Hogg had recently been one of the more frequent guests there. On location in Australia, they grew even closer. A former girlfriend of Snowdon's from *Vogue* magazine said: "Lucy is the girl in his life."

It was at this time when the Snowdons were so obviously living separate lives that Rupert Murdoch decided to use his top-selling British Sunday paper, the *News of the World,* to re-kindle public interest in the state of their marriage. Murdoch, an immensely successful Australian press tycoon who has gone on to launch or re-launch major newspapers on three continents, simply did not want or care about losing the knighthood that he might otherwise have eventually expected to receive for "services to the British press." He had already rejected the offer of one from Australian Prime Minister Gough Whitlam. Murdoch *did* care, though, about selling newspapers, and on March 2 and March 9, 1975, he published two articles in the *News of the World* which went further than anything yet printed in Britain in suggesting that their marriage had broken down. One of their close friends was quoted as saying: "They have reached a compromise. Without too much of a public show of disharmony, they have agreed to disagree in certain areas and go their separate ways.

"Once Tony tried to walk a sort of tightrope between his Royal activities and his work. Now he has quite clearly chosen which side he truly prefers and gets on with it.

"He likes to be the breadwinner, and he most definitely is. He earns about £50,000 per year from his work, which is a comfortable improvement on Margaret's £35,000 civil list allowance."

Another friend described their marriage now as "a special relationship." The differences between them could result in some unpleasant scenes. For example, Snowdon had bought an American painting that he thought highly of, but to which Margaret took the most instant and violent dislike. In the ensuing argument, she refused to have it displayed openly in Kensington Palace. Snowdon subsequently had it hung in the lavatory, and told Margaret to look at it there at her leisure "and learn to appreciate it."

The articles pointed out the amount of time that the Snowdons had spent apart from each other, and that this March was the third year in a row that she had missed his birthday due to holidaying in Mustique. Margaret offered the lame excuse: "Neither of us sets much store by birthdays."

In these *News of the World* articles, Roddy was brought into the Royal picture by a national newspaper for the first time. His visit to Mustique the previous year was described as having led to speculation in foreign newspapers that he was the cause of another rift between Margaret and Snowdon. It was admitted that some of their friends had questioned the wisdom of Margaret's choice of escort in recent years, but Margaret was said to have insisted that her choice of guests was a purely private matter, which should not be influenced by "malicious rumours."

For his part, when Roddy was asked about the visit to Mustique, he was hasty—perhaps over-hasty—to explain that there was no question of there being any romance between himself and Princess Margaret. "I think very few people would turn down an offer to holiday with the Queen's sister," he said. "I hope it won't be misunderstood, as I certainly don't want to find myself the centre of a scandal that doesn't exist."

In the second of their two articles, the *News of the World* exhumed several hoary stories about Snowdon's affairs with various women, in particular that of his thirteen-month affair with Jackie Rufus-Isaacs, by now married to Mark Thomson. This affair, which had ended in 1971, had been typical in that Snowdon insisted on absolute and total discretion from his lady friend. As a friend said: "She got fed up with having to sit in the back seat of a car, hidden away. She wanted to have fun, and show off her super bloke." When Jackie naively attempted to break out of this cloak of secrecy, Snowdon coldly cut her out of his life. He had frequently acted in this way. A friend described meeting him in New York:

138

"He was sitting with a lovely girl and waved for me to join them. In a way it was quite remarkable because we chatted for at least ninety minues and not once did she attempt to say a word.

"Though in way, it was typical of him, because, however innocent, he hates his name being linked with that of another woman."

These articles, pointed as they were, brought no immediate response from either Margaret or Snowdon. They both failed to recognise the potential danger to their marriage of Rupert Murdoch's blithe disregard for staid Fleet Street convention ("Don't knock the Royal Family, they can't hit back").

Margaret continued to see Roddy quite openly, and Lucy Lindsay-Hogg, filming in Australia, remained constantly at Snowdon's elbow. Not that life was entirely trouble-free. In Snowdon's absence, Margaret was reported to be worried about the possibility that her 13-year-old son Viscount Linley might not pass the entrance examination to Eton, his father's old school. One of her friends said:

"Princess Margaret talked to everyone about it. It was her main worry throughout the year. She told me his schoolmaster has said David had no chance of passing for Eton, and that really upset her.

"She describes David as being 'Not conducive to learning' or 'Academically a bit unsharp.' But she was determined he should go to Eton, and arranged for him to spend a year with a crammer near Windsor."

Perhaps Margaret's concern was coming a little late in the day. Never a particularly devoted mother, her romantic involvement with Roddy in addition to her frequent and extended trips abroad had resulted in an even greater neglect of her children. The opportunistic Snowdon had even, in November of 1974, attempted to use the children's welfare as a further argument against Margaret continuing to see Roddy.

Yet in March 1975, Margaret could address a meeting of the National Society for the Prevention of Cruelty to Children on the plight of children left on their own. "The increasing number of children being left alone is a disturbing trend," said the

Princess. "We are concerned not only with the purely physical hazards to which a child may be exposed, but also the mental and emotional dangers."

Snowdon returned at the beginning of April, after a nine-week absence, and was furious to find that, despite his instructions—which had at least interrupted the flow of the relationship in the early months of the year— Margaret was still seeing Roddy. Nor was he pleased when Linley, despite his mother's last minute efforts, failed the Eton entrance examination a week or two later. Rather swiftly, Snowdon and Margaret announced that both their children would start going to school the following September at the £1,344 per year Bedales co-educational boarding school in Hampshire. Bedales was regarded as being one of the more progressive of the English public schools, and the Snowdons were trying to make the best of an awkward situation.

With that problem taken care of, Margaret took an unexpected step. She spent the last weekend of May as a house guest at Llanfair, the Monmouthshire home of Roddy's father, Colonel Harry Llewellyn. Colonel Harry, affectionately known as "Foxhunter" after the horse he had ridden to an Olympic Gold medal at Helsinki in 1952, is a figure of some local importance. He owns a 2,000 acre estate, is Deputy Lieutenant of Monmouthshire, and has done much to promote sport and tourism in Wales. He is an eminently respectable person, and by visiting his house with Roddy, Margaret was able to dispel much of the aura of secrecy and furtiveness that Snowdon had hitherto forced upon the couple. She had, in fact, now become "a friend of the family," a sure indication if one were needed that Margaret intended their relationship to be placed on an even more solid footing.

Just one month later, with Snowdon again off to Australia for the BBC, still with Lucy Lindsay-Hogg, Roddy was invited to take part in an experiment that was to give his affair with Margaret an added *piquance*.

A group of eight upper-class young people in their late twenties and early thirties had bought Surrendell Farm, a 47-acre plot in the Wiltshire countryside, for £40,000. They acquired a shambling, dilapidated Jacobean manor house which had not been lived in for more than twelve years, together with an enormous amount of uncurtailed shrubbery which blocked the entire front entrance. To make the house habitable, not to mention making the farm profitable, was a considerable task, and one in which Roddy found himself heavily and enthusiastically involved.

His designated role was that of head-gardener, and this entailed clearing and caring for the vegetable patch adjacent to the main house. The farm was intended to supply vegetables for the restaurant "Parsenn Sally" in nearby Bath, which the same group of people had bought simultaneously. Besides Roddy, these people included Michael Tickner, decorator and part-owner of the successful trendy Fulham restaurant 'Parsons'; John Rendall, an Australian self-styled "writer"; painter Sarah Ponsonby, the niece of Lord Bessborough; actress Helen Mirren; Rendall's sister Toni Furley; and Prince George Galitzine.

For a variety of reasons each of these people—successful in their different fields—had decided to opt out of the competitive aspects of metropolitan life. A visitor joked to Michael Tickner from an upstairs window in the manor house: "How does it feel to look out of here and think to yourself: 'One-eighth of all this is mine?' Tickner stared blankly at him before replying, with faint condescension: "Actually, we don't think of it in that way."

This enterprise, which Michael Tickner ventured to describe as "a capitalistic commune," was an attempt to combine a wholesome country life with some of those creature comforts not usually to be found in the less affluent variety of commune.

Over the course of the next year the farm developed at a very leisurely pace. Gradually, Roddy's small vegetable patch was turned over, fertilised, and sown with two dozen cabbages. A larger, market-garden size patch began to be cleared on stony ground at another side of the house, but this development was temporarily arrested when Roddy's spade struck a massive brick cistern some six inches below the surface of the soil. Animals were acquired: hens, ducks, pigs and (more for the sake of appearances than for any useful function) a goat that was tethered in the courtyard.

Inside the house, more than a decade of decay made the job of restoring the rooms to a draught-free, comfortable state difficult. They decided to replace many of the ceilings and some of the inside walls, eventually, but in the meantime plugged the more obvious holes, draped a main downstairs room with Indian prints, and made the many adjacent bedrooms as warm, dry and agreeable as possible.

Roddy set about his share of the work with admirable gusto. A lady who had spent a weekend at Surrendell helping him dig the vegetable patch described him as "confident, pleasant and unaffected, especially when compared to his brother. They take it in turns to cook the main meal at the farm, and Roddy's speciality when I was there was spinach soup. Roddy is very much throwing himself into it all, for him it is not a byline in any sense. He never fitted in with Dai's classy City set, but down there at Surrendell he has a very nice room-cum-studio which he is doing up.

"The atmosphere there is extremely easy-going and relaxed, people are dropping in all the time. They are very cheerful, there is a lot of giggling."

Small wonder, then, that when Princess Margaret paid her first visit to Roddy on Surrendell Farm later that summer, she should have been so delighted. Roddy had gained confidence, he took pride in showing her the fruits of his labour and introducing her to his friends on the farm. They, for their part, coming from well-heeled backgrounds, knew very well how to treat Margaret, and were able to give her a taste of their laid-back and relaxed life-style without forgetting for a minute that she was Royalty. They may only just have installed running water, but they were as dutiful in deferring to her and addressing her as 'Ma'am' as any footman at Kensington Palace.

Margaret's first visit to Surrendell was an extraordinary event. Even more extraordinary was her next visit, when, without precedent, she arranged for her private detective to sleep in the neighbouring village of Grittleton so as to be completely alone with Roddy and his friends on Surrendell Farm. The following Saturday morning the people of Grittleton (pop. 348) were surprised by the sight of Princess Margaret shopping in the village. Villagers said, "She wears old clothes and looks like a farmer's wife. She doesn't speak to us."

Margaret enjoyed her visits to Surrendell enormously. Apart from shopping in the village, she was able to muck in with everyone on the farm, to enjoy a degree of earthy informality. The obvious real delight that the members of the farm took in Margaret's presence was very refreshing to her. So at ease did she come to feel in their company that she even went with them one night into Bath, and enjoyed an evening at Parsenn Sally.

By the height of that summer, Margaret and Roddy were deeply involved. On August 8, she took him to Italy with her, to stay at the villa of another old friend, Alessandre d'Urso, on the coast at Conca dei Marini. For three weeks, Margaret was able to indulge them both in the kind of exclusive high-life that remains peculiar to the remnants of the European aristocracy. As a change from the "Jumps-Ups" of Mustique and the communal togetherness of Surrendell, on this holiday Margaret was treated with unctuous sychophancy. Friends did not mix her 11 o'clock gin and tonics here, they were brought by servants. The fact that Roddy was now accepted even in this rarified atmosphere was a considerable achievement. Alessandre d'Urso's guests were charmed by this blond young man's modesty and lack of pretension. Margaret's description of life at Surrendell was received with delight by the guests, conjuring up visions of a bucolic paradise in the heart of the English countryside. Roddy's stock rose still higher.

Back in Britain, at the start of the children's summer holidays, Snowdon took Viscount Linley and Lady Sarah north to Balmoral. He spent a bare eight days with them there, the first appreciable amount of time that he'd spent with them in six months, before leaving on a business trip to the States.

During this stay at Balmoral, Snowdon made good use of his time. He made it quite clear for the first time to Queen Elizabeth how strongly he felt about the continuing association of his wife with Roddy Llewellyn, even going so far as to raise the awesome subject, divorce.

Margaret was due to return from Italy for her birthday on August 21, and Snowdon was fobbed off with the reply that some attempt would be made then to make Margaret see reason and be at least a bit more *discreet* in behaviour. It was at about this time that Roddy's father, when asked what future he saw for Roddy and Margaret, replied: "None, I fear. I can only hope he grows out of her." Colonel Harry, who might normally have been expecting a knighthood in the near future for his considerable service to the local community, received strong hints from sources close to the Palace that this knighthood might be placed in jeopardy by his son's relationship with the Queen's sister. Subsequently, on Roddy's return from Italy, Colonel Harry attempted to persuade his son to stop seeing Margaret.

All to no avail. Margaret, after her return, continued to see Roddy, and in October she even spent the weekend again with him at Surrendell. She had if anything become even more complacent about her public image, as was illustrated by her behaviour at the Savoy Grill on October 10. This celebrated old London restaurant was re-opening after an eighteen month gap, and eighty-four distinguished guests were invited to sample a superb lunch at one o'clock precisely. Margaret did not arrive until 1:20 P.M., by which time "the chef was pacing up and down wringing his hands." Having arrived, she surprised the company by refusing the selected wines and drinking only gin and tonics throughout a delicate and carefully prepared lunch—which she ate, according to one observer, "as though she hadn't seen a decent meal for a week."

Margaret then set off on her ill-fated 13-day solo tour of Australia. From the beginning, nothing went smoothly. Union problems, and complaints in the Australian press about the cost of Margaret's travelling expenses were followed by the gruesome death of the curator of the Victoria State Art Gallery, Brian Finemore, bludgeoned to death a few hours before he was to show Margaret around his Gallery. (Margaret was not told about the murder until later.) In the middle of the tour she displayed a singular lack of regal grace by bringing it to a halt, complaining that her feet were sore and declining to see any further exhibits.

The following month, Margaret's public image was not enhanced by the discovery that senior pupils at her childrens' school, Bedales, had been caught in possession of the hallucinogenic drug LSD. The headmaster told a press conference: "There is no drugs problem . . . the incident could not have affected the Royal children." Nevertheless, he ordered a full investigation to see if any more drugs were hidden in the 420 pupil school, and was planning lectures on the dangers of drug-taking.

That winter, Snowdon finally decided to start moving out of Kensington Palace. He no longer seemed to care about keeping up the pretence, and started looking for somewhere else suitable to use as a base.

By the end of 1975, the seriousness of the rift between Margaret and Snowdon was such that both of their lawyers had been instructed to find the most convenient way of formalising a Royal separation. Snowdon had insisted on this, and by doing so, he put the whole affair on a different level. It was as if, frustrated and exasperated by the uncertainty and procrastination of the Palace, he was finally letting them know that he would no longer put up with this absolutely intolerable situation.

Snowdon realised that the Royal Family's horror of divorce was so strong and deeply implanted that there was little chance of them allowing Margaret and him to get one. So, denied divorce, Snowdon had to settle for the next best thing. In consultation with his solicitor Lord Goodman (who has represented so many well-connected people, from Prime Minister Harold Wilson down), Snowdon discovered a way that would minimise any embarrassment to the Royal Family caused by the breakdown of his marriage. This would be done by instigating a "legal separation." The effect of a legal separation would be similar to that of a divorce, except that the parties would *not* be free to re-marry.

The advantage of a legal separation is that arrangements can be made about money and children without going to court. Furthermore, after two years, under its terms, it is relatively easy for one of the parties, *with the consent of the other*, to obtain a divorce. Given the Royal Family's position on divorce, Margaret would be unlikely to give any such consent, but in that case the law then allows a divorce to take place *without any consent being required*, after a period of five years separation.

Snowdon saw this formula as the best means to disentangle himself from Margaret without getting them both involved in the normal procedure of divorce. Any such divorce would embarrass the Queen in her position as Supreme Governor of the

Church of England, and undoubtedly attract the disapproval of influential church leaders and others for upsetting the established principles of Christian family life which the Snowdons by their marriage of 1960 had sworn to uphold. Snowdon insisted, however, that he was not prepared to wait indefinitely for this legal process to be instituted.

At the beginning of February 1976, Margaret nevertheless flew out for her annual holiday in Mustique, once again taking with her Roddy Llewellyn. When Roddy said that he couldn't afford the full first class air-fare from London, rather than travel separately they flew together on a slightly cheaper flight via Luxembourg to Barbados.

It was on this visit that Australian press magnate Rupert Murdoch finally succeeded in obtaining the visual evidence of the liaison between Margaret and Roddy Llewellyn that the whole world's press had been looking for over the last two years. On February 22, his British Sunday newspaper, the *News of the World*, published on its front page a fuzzy photograph of Margaret and Roddy sitting side by side at a beachside table on the island enjoying a drink. The accompanying article—headlined "MARGARET AND THE HANDSOME YOUNG COURTIER"—described how each day "Margaret and Roddy walk arm-in-arm on the beach," and carefully reported that "Roddy rubs sun-tan oil on her bronzed shoulders. She can suddenly look radiant in a way the public have not seen for a long time." The only time the reporter said he saw Roddy leave Margaret's side was when tourist cameras were pointed in their direction.

This photograph and story was a tremendous scoop for Rupert Murdoch, who was able to sell the package all over the world. A prominent Fleet Street journalist describes how Murdoch achieved it: "The *News of the World* sent a man under false pretences. He was from *News International*, which is Murdoch's company. His name was Ross Waby, and he is a New Zealander you see. He rang up the Mustique booking agency, and said: 'Me and my wife would like to come for a holiday,' so he booked in for a week and paid the money. And on a New Zealand passport, no one suspected him of anything.

146

"He went around like a tourist for a week, with his Kodak Instamatic, and you can see didn't take a good photograph. He was simply sitting at an adjacent table, with his camera in front of him pointed casually at Roddy and Margaret, and since he couldn't put the camera to his eye he simply banged down the shutter with his palm occasionally, and hoped for the best.

It cost Murdoch about £2,000—that's £60 a day all-in plus the flight down there. He was very lucky to get the photograph. Colin Tennant is very alert to newspaper people, he can tell an English journalist a mile off."

On the very Sunday that this photograph and report appeared in the *News of the World,* an irate Lord Snowdon arrived at Windsor Castle and insisted on seeing the Queen. In the presence of one or two other members of the family, he wildly threatened to "talk publicly about his marriage problems," and spoke again of sueing for divorce. Not surprisingly, Snowdon got little satisfaction at Windsor, apart from the dubious pleasure of acting the part of the cuckolded husband and complaining bitterly about being "humiliated and made to look ridiculous." He left the Castle convinced that if he was to see results quickly, he would have to take the matter into his own hands.

On March 2, Margaret flew back to London alone. For the sake of discretion, Roddy had gone on to Barbados, where he stayed for a few days at his father's house. Before returning to London, he picked up a faded copy of the February 22 *News of the World.* Seeing that compromising photograph for the first time, he "waved it in front of the other passengers' noses, shrieking, 'This picture is me, *me!*'" When he got back to England, Roddy was kept well away from the public eye, first at the London flat of City businessman (and brother Dai's employer) Claude Franck, and then at Llanfair Grange where his father insisted that Roddy keep a low profile.

When Roddy returned, however, to a warm welcome at Surrendell Farm a few days later, he laughingly referred to the events of the last few weeks as "The Roddy Horror Show," and sported a T-shirt with the words "RODDY FOR P.M." printed on it. He was given a welcome-home party at Parsenn Sally, which continued until 7 A.M. back at the Farm. The last few hours were devoted entirely to conversation about Princess Margaret.

In London, Snowdon, who had by now based himself at his mother's, the Countess of Rosse's house at 18 Stafford Terrace, off Kensington High Street, had come to a decision. He was due to leave London on March 16 for a major photographic exhibition in Sydney, Australia, and would be out of the country for three weeks. Snowdon had been told that the Palace was holding back any announcement of a separation between himself and Margaret until after their children were back for the Easter holidays, "when there would probably be further discussions and arrangements." Snowdon no longer trusted these protestations. He could see an endless run of "further discussions and arrangements," and he was no longer prepared to put up with it.

Consequently, on the eve of his departure for Australasia, he told his old friend Jocelyn Stevens, the Managing Director of the Express group of newspapers, to go ahead and print in the *Daily Express* that Snowdon and Margaret were shortly to be legally separated, that the subject had been discussed by the Royal Family, and that the Queen had given her consent to this break-up of a Royal marriage. In doing this, Snowdon took a lot of people by surprise: Margaret, the Palace, and all the other newspapers— who quickly picked up the story and headlined it in their second editions. Since the Palace could not deny the *Express*'s story, its Press Office was obliged to issue embarrassed statements: "Obviously, the situation has been discussed by the Royal Family, but I am not in a position to say whether a decision has been reached." Sir Martin Charteris, the Queen's private secretary, went even further: "I don't in truth know what is going to happen. I can assure you that nothing immediate is going to happen— but you could ask what 'immediate' means." This last statement reflects the weary relief felt by the Palace now that, at last, the story was blown. They no longer had any secret to sit upon.

Snowdon, as intended, was in flight between Heathrow Airport and New Zealand when the story broke. He'd had one minor scare when his aeroplane was forced to turn back from the end of the Heathrow runway because of a warning klaxon in its cockpit. Briefly, Snowdon waited in the departure lounge, surrounded by pressmen who—fortunately for him—were as yet unaware of next day's *Daily Express* lead story. They simply asked him the standard questions, and received the standard replies: "I have always made it my policy to talk about photography and films—about my work—but never to discuss my private life. I love my work, just love it . . . although I sometimes feel like a yo-yo." Oddly, when the areoplane's minor fault had been fixed, he left telling reporters that the wait had been made worthwhile by the orange juice and coffee, and that he was "a very old man." Two weeks before, he had celebrated his 46th birthday.

Obviously, media attention in the wake of the *Express* story was focused on Surrendell Farm, which found itself besieged. On the following day, Roddy drove his blue Ford transit van out a back gate, across seeded fields, and sought sanctuary from pursuing pressmen at actress Diane Cilento's farm five miles away. On arriving at Miss Cilento's house he threw a blanket over his head before rushing indoors. Back at Surrendell, John Rendall—who had increasingly assumed the role of commune leader—had unsuccessfully attempted to divert the press by driving out of the farm's front gate in an orange Volkswagen. With Roddy safely stowed away, Rendall calmed down sufficiently to confide to the press: "Roddy is lying low. He is keeping in touch with the Palace. He will know the right time to reappear." Richard Courtauld added: "You can see the difficulty he is in. He is keeping out of the way so that no one can get at him." Michael Tickner rather superfluously pointed out: "Roddy's not here—he went away last night."

In London, there was little more for the press to cover. The Palace's March 18 statement was "No statement will be made today," but the *Express* kept the issue alive by re-publishing the *News of the World* photograph of Roddy and Margaret on Mustique, under the inspired headline:

"THE PICTURE A HUSBAND JUST COULDN'T TAKE."

149

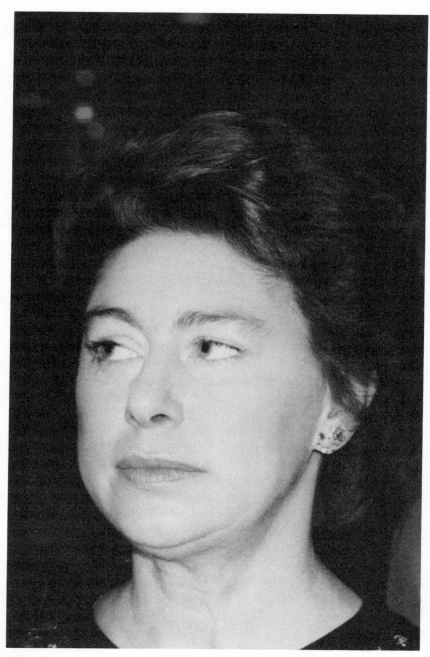

After the separation: Princess Margaret in London, 1976

The following day, at 2:30 P.M., came this simple statement from Kensington Palace:

"HRH the Princess Margaret, Countess of Snowdon, and the Earl of Snowdon have mutually agreed to live apart. The Princess will carry out her public duties and functions unaccompanied by Lord Snowdon. There are no plans for divorce proceedings."

Immediately after this statment had been issued, Margaret left with her children to join her mother and sister for the weekend at Windsor. In Sydney, Snowdon, having successfully warded off the press's questions about his private life for two days, made a statement of his own.

"I am naturally desperately sad in every way that this had to happen," he told a Press conference.

"And I would just like to say three things.

"First, to pray for the understanding of our two children.

"Secondly, to wish Princess Margaret every happiness for her future.

"Thirdly, to express, with the utmost humility, my love, admiration and respect I will always have for her sister, her mother, and indeed her entire family.

"Thank you, ladies and gentlemen."

The third statement was delayed. John Rendall told journalists at Surrendell Farm that "Roddy will be issuing a statement through the Press Association." It was due on Monday 22nd. This of course, led to speculation that Roddy was being gagged. On Saturday, March 20, Kensington Palace denied that any statement by Roddy had been vetoed. They admitted, however, that Roddy *had* telephoned Lord Napier, Princess Margaret's private secretary, on Thursday or Friday for "advice."

Over the weekend Roddy drafted a provisional statement

Lord Snowdon at his Sydney press conference: "I am naturally desperately sad"

with the help of Anthony Shaffer (author of the hit play and film *Sleuth*), and some of his friends from Surrendell. Roddy then took this to his father at Llanfair Grange, who "considered it too full and frank," and the final short statement, a model of discretion, was prepared by Colonel Llewellyn. On Tuesday 23, a day late, this statement was handed, together with a soulful-looking photograph of Roddy, to a Press Association representative by a third party (who would not reveal Roddy's hiding place) under cloak-and-dagger conditions. It read: "I am not prepared to comment on any of the events of last week. I much regret any embarrassment caused to Her Majesty the Queen and the Royal Family, for whom I wish to express the greatest respect, admiration and loyalty.

"I thank my own family for their confidence and support, and I am very grateful for the help of my friends at the farm who, with myself, share a common interest in restoring a house to its original order and beauty, and in farming land which it is hoped will provide food for our Parsenn Sally restaurant in Bath.

"Could we please be permitted by the media, who have besieged us, to carry on with our work and private lives without further interference?"

On the same day, both Roddy's father and President Idi Amin of Uganda issued statements. Harry Llewellyn's was vague and non-committal, speaking as it did of a "young man powerless to defend himself." Amin's statement contained a little more flavour. Addressed to Snowdon, it said that the breakdown of his marriage to Princess Margaret "will be a lesson to all of us men to be careful not to marry ladies in very high positions."

On the weekend prior to all this activity, Margaret was maintaining her low profile at Windsor, dutifully joining her family at all of the little, local functions—such as morning service at All Saints' Church, near Royal Lodge. In Sydney, Snowdon predictably began to pick up the pieces of his "shattered" life. Equally predictably, he did it with some style. Sporting a smart beige safari suit, and strolling through the Sydney sunshine with attractive widow Eve Harman, editor of Australian *Vogue*, he told a reporter of the strain he had been under: "As you can understand, the last few days have not been easy for me. Some people might have thought that my public statement was rather amusing. I can tell you it was not. It was the hardest thing I have ever had to do in my life. Please, you must understand that."

Meanwhile, that same weekend Rupert Murdoch's *News of the World* was not letting a good story go to waste. It published the frankest resume of the affair yet to be seen in the press. A series of quotes from various sources built up the picture of a one-dimensional affair that could have come straight out of the pages of a third-rate romantic novel. "They have changed completely, and so much for the better. They have turned each other into happy people. They have saved each other's lives. They are both emotional, and if they feel like having a bloody good blub, they sit down and have one. Later they feel marvelous. Apart from that, they have the same tastes, like the same people, and all that sort of thing. It wouldn't matter if she were a Queen herself and Roddy was a dustman—they would still be as loving together."

Roddy was said to have been responsible for changing Margaret from being the most unpopular member of the Royal Family—known behind her back as The Bitch—into an agreeable, easy-going person. This cameo version of their relationship undeniably made good copy, but distorted the truth behind the affair. The *News of the World* made it appear, for instance, that the sole cause of the break-up of the Snowdon's marriage was Margaret's falling in love with her soul-mate, Roddy Llewellyn. Colonel Harry Llewellyn was more accurate in declaring that it was not purely Roddy who was responsible for the separation: "The inopportune announcement of the break-up of Lord Snowdon's and Princess Margaret's marriage was a real surprise to Roddy and to us. As far as the holiday picture is concerned, any man could be sitting alongside another man's wife having a drink, but nobody would read anything into that."

Colonel Harry was, in fact, absolutely right, although Snowdon in Sydney was still protesting loudly that he had known nothing of the separation announcement—"I was in mid-air on my way to Australia when things started to happen." The fact remained that it was Snowdon's decision to leak the news of separation discussions to Jocelyn Stevens and the *Daily Express,* and to use the holiday photograph—"I could no longer stand to be publicly humiliated and made to look a fool"—as a device, which precipitated the Royal separation.

The exact nature of the relationship between Roddy Llewellyn and Margaret has never been as clear as the newspapers, Lord Snowdon and the rest of the world might have liked to believe. Even close friends don't pretend to know exactly what goes on between them. On the weekend following the separation announcement, a lady who was a guest at Surrendell met Roddy for the first time and described him as "very, very attractive." She said "he seems very nice and unaffected by it all," but added that he seemed "asexual, not a very passionate type," and that Margaret did not appear to be "the love of his life, he didn't seem to be overbothered if he couldn't see her for a couple of months. There are boys like this, and some women find them very attractive. I didn't actually see the sheets, but I don't imagine they do it five times a night."

Another, more intimate friend, phrased similar sentiments in a different way: "Red-hot passion? Well—I don't think it's a passion.

"I don't know what goes on between the sheets. You know, she's a very lonely lady. She doesn't have the opportunity that you and I have of getting to meet people. Nor does she have the opportunity to take people out. Therefore, when she finds someone that she gets on with, she tends to, you know, hang on to them. It's company, that's all. The poor lady is alone a lot, and she's very difficult to get on with.

"He's just a nice, effete young man. It's quite a difficult role for him to have to play. A couple of years ago, Roddy disappeared and Margaret, distraught, made what amounted to be a cri de coeur."

Perhaps the final sour comment on this cataclysmic liaison was made by Roddy's father, Colonel Harry "Foxhunter" Llewellyn, when he was asked what he thought of Princess Margaret:

"You mean Roddy's new friend? Well, it makes a change from his usual Italian waiters."

AFTERWORD

Following the announcement of the separation, a colleague of Lord Snowdon—or Tony Armstrong-Jones, as he now wishes to be called—said "There is no chance of Tony and Margaret getting back together. I think they both feel that too much has happened." Their paths have crossed twice: at the confirmation of their son, Viscount Linley, and his cousin Prince Andrew in April 1976; and later the same month at the Queen's 50th birthday party at Windsor Castle. Since then, they have gone their separate ways.

Princess Margaret has returned to the round of royal functions, liberally breaking her work schedule with lengthy holidays. In July she went to Spain, in December she returned to Mustique for Colin Tennant's lavish 50th birthday celebrations. In between these two, she had been weekending with Roddy Llewellyn in Scotland, at the highland home of Major John Wills, and at the Peebleshire estate of Colin Tennant where they had first met. In fact, despite the Palace's strong disapproval, Margaret and Roddy have kept in constant touch. Just eleven weeks after the announcement of separation, Roddy was openly driving away from Kensington Palace in the early hours of the morning, having just spent five hours in Margaret's company. "She is still," said a friend of the Tennants, "clearly very close to Roddy." A friend of Roddy's adds: "They never really parted. They went their separate ways as a smokescreen. Everything is the same as it was."

Tony Armstrong-Jones, temporarily homeless on his return to London in April, lodged both with his mother and with his old friend Jeremy Fry before buying for £70,000 a five-bedroom Kensington mansion in October. He then jetted all over the world on a seven-week tour, time spent mainly in the preparation of a new book of photographs—although he also helped sell £60,000 worth of flat-bottomed boats, designed and built by Jeremy Fry's engineering company. Towards the end of the year, his old interest in the plight of the disabled came again to the public attention, when the report of a working party that he had chaired was published, and he chose to break his six-month silence to give a BBC television interview on the subject of the severely disabled.

Roddy Llewellyn, after lying low for a few weeks following the announcement of the separation, returned to Surrendell. Unfortunately, the commune gradually disintegrated until by August all that was left was for Michael Tickner to say: "There was a row among us all. I guess it is now the end of the commune." Parsenn Sally, the commune's restaurant, was wound up with debts of £28,000. By the autumn term of 1976, Roddy had enrolled to study horticulture at Merrist Wood Agricultural College in Surrey, and was lodging with a vicar. "He told his father and me," said Mrs. Llewellyn, "that he was fed up with the commune because he had to do all the work. It really wasn't fair on the boy."

PHOTO CREDITS

Page 15: Keystone Press Agency Ltd.

Page 21: (top) Camera Press London. (bottom left) Keystone Press Agency Ltd. (bottom right) Keystone Press Agency Ltd.

Page 38: Photograph by Dorothy Wilding, Camera Press London.

Page 46: Keystone Press Agency Ltd.

Page 50: Keystone Press Agency Ltd.

Page 57: Camera Press London.

Page 63: Rex Features Ltd., Photograph by Gerard Decaux—Sipa Press

Page 68: Photograph by Tom Blau, Camera Press London.

Page 81: Study by Antony Armstrong-Jones, Camera Press London.

Page 87: (top) Camera Press London. (bottom) Camera Press London.

Page 100: (top left) Camera Press London (Tom Blau/Peter Mitchell) London (top right) Camera Press London (bottom) Photograph by James Reid, Camera Press London

Page 115: Camera Press London

Page 117: (top) Camera Press London (bottom) Photograph by Armando Pietrangeli, Rex Features Ltd.

Page 120: Photograph by Robert Whitaker, Camera Press London (Inset) Keystone Press Agency

Page 135: Photograph by Penny Tweedie, Camera Press London

Page 150: Associated Press London

Page 152: Camera Press London